THE BEGINNER'S GUIDE TO

HOMESCHOOLING

By Patrick Farenga

Published by:
Holt Associates/GWS
2380 Massachusetts Ave.
Suite 104
Cambridge, MA 02140
(617) 864-3100
www.holtgws.com

First printing 10/95
Second printing 4/96
Second edition 12/97
Third printing with updated resource list, 6/99
Third edition, 4/1/2000

Cover Photo Credit: Melody Becher
Front and Back Cover Design: Maria Whitworth

ISBN 0-913677-17-5

Library of Congress Cataloging-in-Publication Data

Patrick Farenga, 1957-
    The beginner's guide to homeschooling/by Patrick Farenga.—3rd ed.
        p. cm.
    Includes bibliographical references (p.) and index.
    ISBN 0-913677-17-5
    1. Home schooling—United States. I. Title.

LC40 .F35 2000
371.04'2—dc21

00-020312

CONTENTS

INTRODUCTION 1
John Holt 3
Growth of homeschooling 5

WHAT IS HOMESCHOOLING LIKE? 8
Socialization 8
Demographics 12
Working parents 12

HOW HOMESCHOOLING WORKS 17
A Typical Day 17
Being a qualified teacher 24

PLANNING YOUR YEAR 29
Curriculum 33
What will we do? 34
Scheduling 40
But I Can't Teach That! 43
Record Keeping 48
Evaluation 56
Standardized Testing 57
Portfolio Evaluations 57
Progress Reports 58
Performance Assessments 58
College & Work 59
College Admissions List 62

APPENDIX ONE 63
Homeschooling before 1977 63

APPENDIX TWO 75
Correspondence schools & curricula 75
Helpful private schools 77

HOMESCHOOLING ORGANIZATIONS:
State & Local 80
National Groups 96
Special Interest Groups 98
Groups Outside the U.S. 99
Other organizations 104

APPENDIX THREE 107
LEARNING MATERIALS AND RESOURCES:
Arts, Crafts, Films 107
Books, Games, & Materials 108
Computers & Electronics 112
Education 112
Foreign Languages 113
Music 115
Opportunities, Activities 115
Parenting 118
Science & Nature 118
Social Studies 120
Special Needs 122
Writing 123

INDEX 124

ACKNOWLEDGEMENTS

I have been helped over the years by the thousands of homeschooled children and their parents that I have met in person and through the pages of *Growing Without Schooling* magazine. Their commitment to try something different has helped me gain confidence about what ordinary parents can do to affect positive social change.

This book would not be possible without the good humor and prodding of Phoebe Wells, who consistently told me to keep working on this book; the substantial help and support of Dick Westheimer; the top-notch thinking and writing done by my colleague Susannah Sheffer; and the combined efforts of Suzanne MacDonald and Meredith Collins for making sure my writing and directories are presented correctly and accurately.

Most importantly, I want to thank my wife, Day, and my children for their love, and for turning homeschooling theories into practice every day of the year for me.

A NOTE ABOUT BOOK REFERENCES

I frequently mention books in the text, but I do not give publisher information. Instead I provide author and title, which is enough information for most librarians, bookstores, and internet search engines to locate books today. I do, however, provide addresses in the text for a few hard-to-find books. Unless noted, all books mentioned in the text are in print as of the year 2000.

Also unless noted, all quotations from homeschoolers come from various issues of the magazine I publish, *Growing Without Schooling*.

INTRODUCTION

I never thought I would homeschool my children when I came to work at *Growing Without Schooling* magazine in 1981. I viewed work at Holt Associates, the publishers of *Growing Without Schooling,* as a way to gain office skills, not as a place where my ideas of education would change. "After all," I reasoned in my early twenties, "I could always become a teacher if I don't like office work." But over the course of my frequent exposure to homeschooled children, their parents, a wide variety of teachers, writers, and the late John Holt, I was able to convince myself, and my wife (no small task there!), that homeschooling not only made sense in terms of learning academics, but also, and especially, from the viewpoint of how we wanted to help our children learn about living in our world. Neither my wife nor I had particularly bad schooling experiences; we both were sociable, good-to-average students. But we did want a different—and to us, richer—experience for our children than that offered by conventional schooling.

Our three girls are ages 13, 10, and 7 at the time I am writing this, and two of them stopped homeschooling for periods of time to attend public school. Lauren, our oldest, completed sixth grade and then decided she wanted to homeschool again; Audrey, our youngest, wanted to try first grade, which she did for five weeks before she declared she wanted to come home. Audrey was too bored in school, though she loved her teacher and classmates. She realized she could still love and see them even if she didn't attend school with them. Miss Reppucci, her teacher, was openly supportive of my wife about homeschooling. When Audrey decided to leave school, Miss Reppucci made a point of inviting her to school plays and functions so they could all stay in touch. The stereotypes of schools and homeschoolers being at odds with one another have a definite basis in reality but there is also the reality my family has experienced, that schools and homeschoolers can cooperate for the benefit of all.

This book will help you see that there are many ways to teach and learn with your children other than by purchasing traditional school materials and then using them with your family. This is not to say such materials can not be useful—indeed you will find references throughout this book to help you purchase such materials if you wish—but, I feel, they need to be used judiciously and not become the tail that wags the dog. When you homeschool you can change and adapt things to suit your children's interests and family schedules; no matter what your curriculum is or what your homeschooling law is, you do not need to plan out precisely what you are going to do over the entire year. Remember, there is no national curriculum for anyone—schoolchildren or homeschoolers—so even schoolteachers do not have to follow a completely regimented plan. This is changing as individual states, such as my own, Massachusetts, create "high stakes" testing, hoops all children must jump through to receive a state accredited high school degree. However, homeschools and private schools do not have to duplicate public school methods or curricula, and they both can have different educational goals, schedules, and accredited diplomas. As homeschooling parents you have even more flexibility than most classroom teachers to change, adapt, or delay introducing materials or approaches to subject matter in order to help your children learn. This book emphasizes teaching and learning from the perspective of the institution of the family, not from the perspective of the institution of schooling. It emphasizes the simplicity and ease of teaching and learning which come naturally to parents and children who are open to learning in non-school ways. There are many more detailed how-to books for homeschooling, and I recommend some of the ones I like (see pp. 15–16). However, the purpose of this book is to be the first step for people looking into homeschooling, to give a taste of what is possible and get you started with resources for learning without spending a lot of money.

Our company, Holt Associates, and the magazine we publish, *Growing Without Schooling*, have for over 23 years emphasized the value of learning through living (sometimes called "unschooling;" see p. 35). Just as children learn as babies and toddlers to walk and talk without formal instruction they can continue to learn through the incidents of their lives as children and teenagers. Parents provide resources, support, travel, safe environments, guidance, and, when desired, direct instruction for their children. So parents have a very important, though different, role as "teacher" when using the "live and learn" approach to homeschooling. Many alternative schools use these same ideas for teaching and learning, and you can visit them or read about them for "how to" ideas and support (see "Helpful Private Schools," pp. 77–80).

JOHN HOLT

The author and teacher John Holt (1923–1985) founded our magazine *Growing Without Schooling* in 1977 and conceived Holt Associates as a clearinghouse for information about homeschooling. Holt, an experienced fifth grade teacher in private schools, wrote two bestsellers about school reform in the sixties (*How Children Fail* and *How Children Learn*). After working with other reformers to help change schooling in the sixties and seventies, Holt slowly, over the course of two decades, decided that schools could not reform themselves. He recast the problem from being one of schooling to being one of how adults and children can live well together. In the late seventies he wrote, "A life worth living and work worth doing, that is what I want for children (and all people), not just, or not even, something called 'a better education.'" (In *A Life Worth Living: Selected Letters Of John Holt*, ed. Susannah Sheffer; currently out of print.). In his ten books you can see the development of Holt's strong advocacy for children's independent learning and homeschooling, for small community learning centers, and for apprentice/internship work opportunities in lieu of compulsory schooling. It was a difficult journey for Holt both intellectually and emotionally, as he had devoted himself to school reform efforts for many years. But the possibilities of learning and growing without schooling seemed increasingly interesting and exciting to Holt, and he began to turn his attention to families who were actually trying this. In turn, many of these families, who for all sorts of reasons felt that the schools were not working for their children, welcomed Holt's support and insight.

THE GROWTH OF HOMESCHOOLING

In a sense, homeschooling was the primary means of educating our young throughout the world until the advent of universal compulsory schooling about 150 years ago. Further, there have always been people who chose home education over school education (see p. 60 and Appendix One), so it is hardly accurate to call homeschooling a recent phenomenon or fad. When John Holt wrote his book *Teach Your Own: A Hopeful Path for Education* (out of print in the US; available in the U.K.) in 1981 he estimated that perhaps as many as 20,000 children were being taught at home; in 1991, Dr. Patricia Lines of the US Dept. of Education, in a paper, "Estimating the Home Schooled Population," concluded that 350,000 children were taught at home. *Newsweek* (Oct. 7, 1998) estimated at least a million and a half children were being homeschooled that year.

Certainly many other people and publications besides John Holt and *GWS*, such as Raymond and Dorothy Moore, Mary Pride, *The Teaching Home*, and *Home Education Magazine*, influenced the homeschooling movement in its early years, and continue to help it grow. In fact, the most important pioneers of homeschooling are the thousands of men and women (primarily women, I must add!) who not only homeschooled their kids but also organized and led many of the initiatives that have made homeschooling legal in all fifty states and in many other countries as well (see pp. 80–97 for state and country listings of homeschooling support groups).

However, this book is not about the philosophical, historical, and religious underpinnings of the homeschooling movement, but about how you can help your children learn without sending them to school and without doing things exactly as school does. It is here that John Holt has much to offer.

John Holt's unique, probing, and practical books are in large part about how children learn and how adults can help them. Holt felt the separation of living and learning was a major source of the failure of schooling and he did not want to duplicate that failure in homeschooling. His belief that children and adults could learn together, teach one another, and can enjoy life, distinguish him from some homeschooling advocates who want to turn parents into professional teachers and people's homes into private academies.

I came to work at Holt Associates in 1981 as a single man who merely wanted job experience in word processing, not a career in homeschooling. I volunteered at Holt Associates thinking it was just a step for me along the path of a career in corporate America, but the more I learned about word processing, the more I also learned about homeschooling. I had long conversations with John Holt and his colleagues at the office, as well as with homeschoolers, on a daily basis and eventually I came to appreciate homeschooling as a sound educational choice. However, even after three years of working at Holt Associates, when I got married my wife and I were still uncertain if we were going to homeschool our children.

It wasn't a single homeschooling encounter, book, or research paper that convinced us to try homeschooling but rather the accumulation of contacts with homeschoolers whose children were obviously thriving physically, mentally, and spiritually that nudged us in this direction. Some of these parents and their ideas about education were radically different from ours—some followed strict school schedules, others jettisoned school altogether—but there was a commonality my wife and I noticed among all these families: the children were, on the whole, very comfortable in public with their parents and other adults. Indeed, many of the homeschooled children we knew were also fun to be with, good at conversation, and displayed wide-ranging interests and abilities. It was reflecting on our personal experiences with school as students, then on our personal experiences with homeschoolers as adults, as well as thinking about how we would prefer to raise our not-yet-born children, that led my wife and me to realize that there are many different ways to raise a family; many different ways of teaching and learning besides the traditional "read a book and take a test" model school offers. Perhaps I should rephrase this as "do an activity and take a performance assessment" as a way to stay current with the latest school jargon. However, what made us decide to try homeschooling, and what makes us continue to stick with it, is watching other children, and especially our three daughters, learn and grow. As babies and toddlers our children learned to walk, talk, sing, identify colors, reason, and so on without us directly teaching them these things, and as they grow older we see how this process continues. As our children grow they still have questions, needs, and difficulties that my wife and I respond to and sometimes, though not as often as you'd think, we use lessons or other traditional teaching techniques to help our children learn. Of course, you've got to homeschool in a manner you are comfortable with and you may prefer a more schoolish approach than my wife and I do; resources and ideas for that approach are also provided in this book. The point of all this is that you can live and learn comfortably with your children at home and in your community during their compulsory school years without turning your home into a copy of school. Here's how.

WHAT IS HOMESCHOOLING LIKE?

There are as many ways to homeschool as there are families who do it. Indeed, many families discover that what helped one child learn to read or do math doesn't automatically help their other children learn so it is difficult to say for certain, "Homeschooling is like this for everybody..." In general, many parents prefer to start teaching the way they were taught, using regularly scheduled classes and textbooks, and gradually adapt their programs to suit their children's interests and abilities. Shifting away from textbooks to primary source materials, and real life experiences, they draw on other mentors or classes in the community. Some families prefer simply to do "school at home," duplicating school schedules and curricula but screening out objectionable content; there are several correspondence and private schools on pp. 75–80 that will sell you curricula and materials for this type of homeschooling. The way my wife and I prefer to homeschool is by following each of our children's unique growth and development and letting them learn things when they show an interest in learning them (also called "unschooling;" see p. 35). Many families wind up adapting a position in between "school at home" and unschooling; in any case, the decision on what homeschooling will be like for you is yours to make, and it is not an unalterable one.

SOCIALIZATION

When I first started working at *GWS* in 1981, the most common question I was asked by people who heard I supported homeschooling was, "But is it legal?" In 1981 homeschooling was legal in many states, and by the late eighties it was legal in all 50 states. Now, as you can see from looking at the lists starting on page 99, homeschooling is also legal in many other countries, so the most common question homeschoolers are likely to hear in the twenty-first century is: "But how will your children be socialized if they don't go to school?"

For most people, it is the idea that children must be socialized by compulsory schooling rather than family and other institutions, that prevents them from accepting homeschooling as an alternative. They picture homeschooled children as being socially inept because they can only socialize with their parents and siblings; however this is far from true. Research on this topic has consistently shown homeschooled children to be well socialized, which comes as no surprise since the vast majority of homeschoolers seek out or create social opportunities for their children to be with other children and adults besides their immediate family. If we can get away from the age-and-ability-segregated social vision school imposes on us, we can discover the rich social lives young people can have, and have had, outside of school. They can meet and socialize with other people in their neighborhoods, in church, Scouts, 4-H, libraries, community sports and theater, in karate, dance, music, and other classes. Some can even participate in school activities, while others socialize through homeschooling support groups and various clubs they create. See the appendices on homeschooling support groups and the publications mentioned throughout this text for more ideas and stories about how homeschoolers socialize.

Several studies have shown that homeschooled children have a more positive self-concept than their schooled peers, are better behaved in groups, and are at least as well-socialized as schoolchildren. Two research-oriented books that came out in the nineties which discuss socialization and other studies of homeschoolers, in areas such as academic achievement, are: *Homeschooling: Political, Historical, and Pedagogical Perspectives,* ed. J. Van Galen and M. A. Pittman (currently out of print) and *Home Schooling: Parents as Educators* by Mayberry, Knowles, Ray, and Marlow. Anecdotal evidence over the years suggests that children who learn at home and don't go to school are more likely to have friends of different ages and less likely to engage in the cliquish, exclusivist behavior so common in schools.

As a growing number of teenage homeschoolers will tell you, leaving the social life of school is actually a great reason to homeschool. See Chapter Six in Grace Llewelyn's *The Teenage Liberation Handbook* for an excellent presentation of this particular aspect of homeschooling and socialization for teens.

Further, contrary to popular opinion, most homeschoolers do not isolate themselves from those who attend conventional school. Homeschoolers can still be friends with those who go to school, of course. April Johnson and Christina Dubberley, both seventeen, described their relationship this way when talking with Susannah Sheffer, the editor of *Growing Without Schooling*:

> SS: Is there anything hard about a friendship between a homeschooler and someone who goes to school?
> Christina: We don't necessarily see each other regularly. I see my other friends every day, and I don't see April as often.

April: Yeah, I think that's the biggest thing. But I don't feel jealous of Christina's other friends, because she invites me to parties and things like that, and I know a lot of her friends.

Christina: And a couple of my friends have siblings who homeschool, and April knows them.

SS: You know how some people say that, in high school, it's hard to be different, everyone wants to fit in, and all that? I wonder if people ever have that reaction, Christina, when they hear you're friends with someone who is doing something different?

Christina: There are some people who are like that at the high school, who don't like anybody who's different. There definitely are cliques, where you have to dress the same, or act the same. But none of my friends are like that—all of my friends are individualists. If somebody said what you described, though, I would say, "If I were talking to somebody who was exactly the same as me, I might as well be talking to myself, and that would get pretty boring after a while."

SS: What about for you, April? What if some homeschoolers asked why you are friends with someone who goes to school?

April: Some homeschoolers I know do seem to think that kids who go to school are evil, that they're totally out of control. I tell them that there are homeschooling kids who act immature, too. Kids are kids. If they asked me why I was friends with someone who goes to school, I'd say I don't think the school thing is an issue. We're friends because we're friends.

HOMESCHOOLING DEMOGRAPHICS

All sorts of people homeschool. Homeschoolers live in the country, city, suburbs, and in small towns. Some are single-parent families. Some run family businesses, and some parents combine working outside the home with homeschooling. Studies show that homeschooling is primarily done by Caucasian families, who have an average of three children, with one child who is typically younger than school-age, and the mother does most of the homeschooling while the father works. However, the homeschooling movement is growing increasingly diverse as people of many religions, philosophies, and ethnic backgrounds choose to homeschool. In addition to several groups and publications specifically for Christian homeschoolers, there are now groups and newsletters addressing the concerns of Jewish homeschoolers, Muslim homeschoolers, and homeschoolers of color. See pp. 98–99 for addresses of these groups and for other organizations that can lead you to individual families in your local area.

HOMESCHOOLING AND WORKING PARENTS

The issue of balancing work with homeschooling needs to be addressed by each family. For many families, the easiest solution is to have one parent, typically, though not exclusively, the mother, stay at home with the kids while the other parent works. Some parents find they can absorb the loss of one parent's income as a trade-off for being able to homeschool. They may have to cut back on things, but this is something they are willing to do. Others manage to have both parents continue working while they homeschool; your options here will depend a lot on the child's age, level of responsibility your child can handle, and the nature of your work, of course.

Single parents can and do homeschool. The National Homeschool Association (p. 98) maintains a support network for single parents. Typically, single parents find jobs where they can either take their children with them or take their work home. They often rely on older children, sitters, relatives, or close friends to watch their young children when they need to be away for work; teenage homeschoolers are able to be more self-reliant and are often involved in outside activities.

Two-income families homeschool too! My wife and I both work and we find that we can arrange our schedules so I'm at the office or work from home, usually 9AM–5PM, and Day works afternoons or evenings. The hours currently work well for us, suiting Day's theatrical lighting career with my daily business hours. When our children were very young, and Day and I worked together at Holt Associates, they spent quite a bit of time in the office with us, particularly when there were other children around for them to play with. Our oldest daughter, Lauren (now 13), seemed to love the office as a toddler. After "mom" and "dad," the next word she learned was "mail," not surprising since we spend so much time talking about "the mail" at work! Nowadays, our two older daughters are involved in all sorts of activities of their own, and between those activities and the time they spend with friends, neighbors, relatives, and paid babysitters, they aren't in the office much.

One of the first things we noticed as our children got older was that as they became increasingly involved in their own activities, there became less of a need to think of having some-one "watch" them all the time and more of a need to think about scheduling. For instance, when Lauren goes to gymnas-tics classes or when the homeschool drama club holds a rehearsal, it doesn't mean my wife and I need to be there too. We are not the only ones involved in our children's home-schooling, and that has benefits for us as parents, as well as for our children. We do not let our kids do gym or drama in order to give us childcare while we work, but rather because this type of varied life is what homeschooling is for us. Further, it ends up allowing us to work, as well. Parents can gently encourage a child's growth from dependence on their care to indepen-dence as young adults; when kids are older they are often more able to get around on their own, to be by themselves at home or the library, to work with other adults. Try not to think of homeschooling in terms of your kids being home all day or needing parental supervision every minute, because home-schooling naturally encompasses many different activities, as I've described.

There are also two-income families who can't control their work schedules as much as we can. I'm aware of families who deliberately work split shifts (one works days, the other nights), alternate days (four ten-hour days at the office spread out over the week), or have one partner work at home. The creativity and resourcefulness of people who want to home-school is amazing. Mothers on welfare homeschool as do wealthy celebrities: if you want to, you can find a way. We have published many stories about the nitty-gritty details of balanc-ing work with homeschooling in *Growing Without Schooling*.

To get a first-hand overview of what homeschooling can be like for you, attend a homeschooling conference or support group meeting in your area; you may need to try several sources before you find one that suits the way you want to homeschool, but it will be well worth your effort. You may find not only kindred spirits for yourself but also potential friends for your children.

Non-sectarian books and magazines about homeschooling (see pp. 96–98 for magazine addresses):

Family Matters: Why Homeschooling Makes Sense,
    David Guterson
Gentle Spirit magazine
Growing Without Schooling magazine
Home Education Magazine
The Homeschooling Book of Answers, ed. Linda Dobson
The Homeschooling Handbook, Mary Griffith
The Homeschooling Almanac, Mike and Mary Leppert
Taking Charge Through Homeschooling, Larry and
    Susan Kaseman
The Unschooling Handbook, Mary Griffith

Christian books and magazines about homeschooling (see pp. 96–98 for magazine addresses):

Homeschooling Today magazine
Moore Report International magazine
Practical Homeschooling magazine
The Teaching Home magazine
The Homeschool Manual, Ted Wade

The Big Book of Home Learning, Mary Pride
The Christian Home Educator's Curriculum Manual,
    Cathy Duffy

Other books about specific aspects of homeschooling:

*And What About College? How homeschooling leads to admissions to the
    best colleges and universities,* Cafi Cohen
Deschooling Our Lives, ed. Matt Hern
Freedom Challenge: African American Homeschoolers,
    ed. Grace Llewellyn
Real Lives: Eleven Teenagers Who Don't Go To School,
    ed. Grace Llewellyn
*A Sense of Self: Listening to Homeschooled Adolescent
    Girls,* Susannah Sheffer
The Teenage Liberation Handbook, Grace Llewellyn
Writing Because We Love To: Homeschoolers at Work,
    Susannah Sheffer

HOW HOMESCHOOLING WORKS

"WHAT'S A TYPICAL DAY OF HOMESCHOOLING LIKE?"

Thousands of homeschoolers answer this question every day, and they probably give a thousand equally true answers. As most families will tell you, there is no typical day. Certainly you can set up your home as a school, schedule it like school, and teach like in school: resources for purchasing curricula and educational materials are provided on pages 75–80, and on pages 107–123. *The Big Book of Home Learning* by Mary Pride and *The Christian Home Educator's Curriculum Manual* by Cathy Duffy have reviews from a Christian perspective about many curricular packages you can purchase for homeschooling. But if the total "school at home" approach becomes stifling to you or your kids, or if, like many homeschoolers I know, you prefer to move back and forth between imposed lessons and learning from the incidents of every day life on a relaxed, individualized schedule, consider some of these other ways to help your children learn.

Homeschooling children also learn through reading, through conversation, through solitary reflection, through play, through outside classes, through volunteer work and apprenticeships. Typically, children will have some time on their own at home (to read, play, build, draw, write, do a science experiment, work on math), some time with their parents (to get help with any of the above, to talk, to do some kind of focused project together), and some time with others outside the home (in a music class, in Scouts, in a homeschoolers' book discussion group, in a volunteer job at a museum). Some families set aside a part of the day for focused academic work; others do not. Often this varies for each child and the family often adapts its schedule as the children grow and their needs change.

It is important to remember that homeschooling doesn't have to mean that your kids stay at home all day, with only their parents, using school materials. For instance, several times a week we schedule our children to be with other friends, typically, but not exclusively, homeschoolers; we reciprocate at other times during the week. For instance, my wife ran "The Detective Club," a popular meeting held every Wednesday night at our house for eight children: seven homeschoolers and a friend who attends public school. We also make use of field trips, history clubs, French clubs, drama clubs, etc. run by other homeschooling parents. Classes at museums, area library events, religious instruction, and other resources that we find, such as the local gymnastics and dance academies our daughters attend, are also utilized. Indeed, in some states you can probably arrange for your child to take classes in local public schools (it never hurts to ask no matter what state you live in). Some homeschooling support groups have listings of members who are willing to help tutor or converse with children who are interested in learning more about their areas of expertise.

Most importantly, homeschooling allows you to give your children time to explore and think about things on their own. Children who figure things out on their own, for their own purposes, literally do own that knowledge and can build on it. So if your child wants to learn more about, say, marine biology, and you know nothing about the topic (and perhaps have no interest in it at all!), then you can help them by locating books and materials they can read and use on their own; a friendly resource librarian at your local public library can be an invaluable ally in your homeschooling efforts for this reason alone. You can also consider calling pet stores, aquariums, and marine biologists who might be willing to talk to your child, have them visit or volunteer, or simply allow the children to observe what various aspects of marine biology are actually like. So you needn't feel you must know everything before you can teach anything; again, homeschooling doesn't have to be like regular school and you don't have to be like a typical school instructor. Instead you can be a facilitator and guide for your children's travels to areas you don't feel particularly comfortable teaching them.

Madalene Axford Murphy of Pennsylvania writes about how she did this with her son:

> Early on, our son Christian began to reach the limits of his father's and my knowledge in science and math, and it became obvious that these would be major pursuits in his life. At first I cheerfully expanded my own knowledge, learning along with him, but finally I had neither the time nor the interest to keep up with him. We met this situation in a number of ways.
>
> ...We discovered an astronomy group that met one evening a month, and he began to attend meetings. He discovered that one of the founders of the group was giving a twelve-session seminar on astronomy for adults at our local nature center. On the recommendation of the naturalist there

(a friend of his), he was allowed to sign up, though he was only eleven. The first evening, he came home with about ten pages of small print that had to be read for the next class. This was not going to be a warm, fuzzy retelling of myths about constellations with a few facts thrown in here and there about planets and such, but rather a no-holds-barred immersion course in technical astronomy. I was concerned, but Christian wasn't. He plowed through the reading and was disappointed when the classes were over. Did he understand everything? No, nor did many of the adults in the class, but words like "parallax" and "gradient" had become part of his vocabulary and he knew a whole lot more about telescopes and the science of astronomy than he had before.

Another group, the Audubon Society, helped open up several aspects of biology for him... When they started planning their annual Christmas Bird count, Christian and I decided to participate... One of the Society's more active members was a biologist who worked at a nearby fish research lab, and I asked if we could tag along when he went on the bird count. The bird count itself was not a success: periods of freezing rain kept most of the birds out of sight and made me think they were definitely displaying intelligence superior to the humans on that particular occasion...

...But the biggest success of the bird count was the friendship that developed between Christian and Bob, the biologist.

Bob invited Christian on other bird counts and for the last two years has taken him along as a timekeeper/recorder on an intense five-hour government-sponsored survey of birds. Christian has become quite skilled at identifying birds and is even trying to improve his ability to recognize their calls.

The summer after the original bird count, Christian discovered he could volunteer at the fish research lab where Bob worked, and he ended up working two eight-hour days a week... Christian learned a lot about lab techniques and about the amount of tedious work required to get accurate results for a study...

All of these biology activities took place during Christian's "high school" years, a time when homeschooling parents and sometimes children often begin to get a bit more nervous about whether they need to become more traditional, particularly if the children are planning on college. Christian did decide to use textbooks to fill in gaps in his knowledge of science, and activities like those I just described made the textbook knowledge real and useful.

Here are two examples of how families used play and conversation to help their children learn math. Carla Stein of Massachusetts writes:

> I took 51 pieces of typewriter paper and wrote the numbers 0 through 50 on them. We lay them out on the floor, Candy Land style, in

all sorts of loops and turns around the furniture... Then we took turns hopping along the trail, stepping only on numbers that were odd, or even, or divisible by 3, 4, 5, etc... This made for silly fun, especially when the jumps got too long. Then they each got a small stuffed toy and tried to toss the toys onto the right numbers, with lots of misses and shrieking, of course.

Sue Smith-Heavenrich of New York writes:

Some time ago my children were doing "math before breakfast"—a sort of game where they ask each other questions while I get out the cereal and juice. Coulter (who's seven) asked, "What's 1 Toby plus 1 Toby?" Toby, four years old, answered, "Eight."

"No, no," responded Coulter. 'What's 1 Toby plus 1 Toby?"

"Eight!" answered Toby, with more volume and conviction.

Suddenly it dawned on me that he was right. In terms of age, two Tobies is the same as 2 x 4, which is 8. So as I passed out the bowls, I asked if one Toby was equal to 4 years. "Yes," Toby replied. They then began to create equations using their friends' ages: "Does 1 J (9) - 1 K (7) + 1 I (6) = 1 T (4)?" and so on.

I wonder how often "wrong answers" are simply right answers to different interpretations of a question. If the purpose of math is to use symbols to phrase observations about the world, then we need to give our children time to grow up using the language of math, and exploring it. When they began to talk, we did not demand that they pronounce each word correctly or use proper grammar. So, too, I think mathematical thinking needs to grow naturally.

I grew up hating math. I remember my father sitting down with me each evening after dinner to go over flash cards. I feared getting the wrong answer. And so, as my reading and verbal abilities grew, my math skills remained stuck, as I made tortuous progress through workbook after workbook. I never, ever would have asked my sister at the breakfast table, "What's 1 Sue plus 1 Sue?" I simply avoided all math, believing (as my mom said) that I was "mathlexic."

Perhaps this is why I do not "teach" math to my children. We work out our problems, play games with numbers, and use math as a tool in our daily living. Today we were sorting potatoes for market and weighing them. This led to all sorts of interesting math problems. The weight of the bowl we were using to hold the potatoes was 1/4 lb. Often we'd get a bowl full of potatoes that weighed something like 3 3/4 lb. I haven't yet formally taught fractions, but Coulter figured out how much the potatoes weighed, and added different weights together for a total. His comments? "Gee, Mom, this is fun! When are you going to dig more?"

The stories in *GWS*, other homeschooling publications (see pp. 96-98) and in books about homeschooling will give you a much fuller picture of how homeschooling works for different families.

On Being a Qualified Teacher

No state requires you to be a certified teacher. You should remember that you are not teaching a class of thirty children, but just your own children, something you've done already for years. The dynamics of classroom teaching and the tutorial approach you can use in homeschooling are completely different. Your children have large blocks of time with you so their questions can arise naturally and often throughout the course of the day. As any parent knows, young children will ask questions if they aren't conditioned to stop asking them. Just because lots of people put their children in school or, if younger, under professional day care, does not automatically mean that certified professionals are better at nurturing children's learning than uncertified parents.

For instance, a British study, described in *Young Children Learning* by Barbara Tizzard and Martin Hughes, compared working class parents who tape recorded conversations with their four-year-old children to nursery school teachers whose conversations with four-year-olds were also recorded. It revealed that the children who stayed home were persistent and logical thinkers, asking all sorts of questions about a diverse number of topics. The children under the care of professional teachers were more subdued, their conversation with adults mainly restricted to answering questions rather than asking them.

Many wonder how ordinary parents can be as successful as schoolteachers in helping children learn. The Washington Homeschool Research Project's report, *The Relationship of Selected Input Variables to Academic Achievement Among Washington's Homeschoolers*, by Jon Wartes was able to examine this question in some detail. Wartes was able to study a group of homeschooled children whose parents were state certified teachers and children of parents who were not certified. The results showed no difference in their outcomes:

> Examination of the high extreme in teacher-contact (children of certified teachers) produced mixed results. In general, children of teachers did outscore children of non-teachers on the Stanford Achievement Test series. However, this result did not hold when one considers students who have been home-schooled two years or longer. It also did not hold when non-teacher parents having a roughly equivalent level of education to a teacher (sixteen years—PF) were compared. At the opposite extreme, children who had no teacher contact scored, as a group, at the seventieth percentile on national norms. This latter finding suggests that contact with a certified teacher is not a necessary component of academic success. Policy decisions that would, as a general matter, require contact with a certified teacher as a condition to homeschool are not supported by this data.

Many private schools do not require their teachers to be state certified in education, but prefer instead to have teachers who have strong knowledge in the subject they plan to teach. The schools prefer a degree in the field of history, for example, rather than a certificate in education, for a history teacher. Why do these schools not worry about certification? Because they know that enthusiasm for teaching, love of the subject matter, and a commitment to children aren't found only in certified teachers. The same is true in homeschooling.

Correspondence schools, such as The Calvert School and the Home Study Institute (see p. 75) have been providing home study courses for American families abroad and at home for many decades. Alaska created a Centralized Correspondence Study program (CCS) that has been in existence for decades. The state mails a correspondence study program to parents who then administer the materials to their children. There has been no evidence over all this time that homeschooled children using these programs do less well than their schooled peers in Alaska or elsewhere.

A study published in 1999 as *Educating Children at Home* by Dr. Alan Thomas (Continuum Publishing Co., 370 Lexington Ave, NY NY 10017-6550) indicates that late reading among homeschooled children is common. Some children may not learn to read until they are ten or eleven years old, but "as far as could be ascertained, [there is no] no adverse effect on intellectual development, self-worth, or even subsequent attainment in literacy." The "late" readers caught up with and soon surpassed the reading level of their schooled age-mates. Dr. Thomas also notes, in contrast to schoolchildren of the same ages,"in common with most other home educated children, [the late readers] went on to thoroughly enjoy reading." Homeschooling can allow learning to take place at more varying paces than the school schedule allows, giving you and your children lots of time to work on things in different ways from school, and time to obtain different results.

Homeschooling is a new term, but having children learn at home and in the community was the primary means for passing along culture and knowledge until the advent of universal compulsory schooling in our country, barely one hundred fifty years ago. Parents didn't worry about public schools teaching their children everything as we do today, but instead they taught their children what they knew how to do and enlisted other people to help their children learn things they themselves couldn't teach. This is pretty much what you can do if you decide to homeschool today. Homeschooling meets traditional standards; homeschoolers generally test as well as or better than their peers in school. It also meets other standards that many families consider even more important: the children love learning, are able to learn in ways that work for them, and the family remains closely connected.

Parents can grow in many different ways while homeschooling, too. One of the great advantages of homeschooling is that we don't have to be the almighty teacher from whom all knowledge flows forth. If the children do not want to learn something on their own, and you don't know anything about it, you can learn alongside your children, thereby strengthening your relationship with them and modeling the behavior of how one finds answers. John Holt wrote:

> One [person] wrote me a furious letter about GWS, saying "How is a welfare mother with five kids going to teach them how to read?" The answer is, teach them herself. If she can't read, but one of her children can, that child can teach the other children, and her. If none of them can read, they can get a relative, or friend, or neighbor, or neighbor's child, to teach them.
>
> Reading, and teaching reading, are not a mystery. The schools, in teaching the poor (and the rich too) that no one except a "trained" teacher can teach, have done them (and all of us) a great and crippling injury and wrong. A

number of poor countries have had mass literacy programs, often called Each One Teach One, in which as fast as people learn to read they begin to teach others. They found that anyone who can read, even if only fifty or a hundred words, and even if he only learned them recently, can teach those words to anyone else who wants to learn them. Every now and then, in this country, a school, often a city school for poor kids, lets older children, fifth or sixth graders, teach first graders to read. Most of them do a better job than the regular teachers. Quite often, older children who themselves are not very good readers turn out to be the best teachers of all. There is a clear lesson, but the schools don't seem able to learn it, mostly because they don't want to.

...And this may be the place to note that "trained" teachers are not trained in teaching, but in classroom management, i.e., in controlling, manipulating, measuring, and classifying large numbers of children. These may be useful skills for schools, or people working in schools. But they have nothing whatever to do with teaching—helping others to learn things.

PLANNING YOUR HOMESCHOOL YEAR

Broadly speaking, there are three steps you need to take in order to start homeschooling:

1) KNOW YOUR STATE'S LAWS AND REGULATIONS.

Find out what the laws or regulations are in your state by contacting someone who is currently homeschooling in your area. Local homeschooling groups are usually the best source of precise information about how to fulfill the requirements of the law in your state. Many groups have information packets for new homeschoolers which include information about laws and regulations. See the listings on pages 80–96 to locate a group in your state or contact one of the national groups listed on pages 96-98 for some advice.

You can find the actual wording of your state's law under "Compulsory Education" or "School Attendance" in a courthouse or law library, or you can write to your State Department of Education for a copy of the current regulations. In general, some states require you to submit a plan to your local district, some require you to file with the State Department of Education, and some allow you to register your home as a private school.

You do not have to be a certified teacher to homeschool in any state.

In addition to being the best source of current information about laws and regulations, homeschooling support groups can help you meet a lot of people at once and can tell you about local activities. Support groups often have newsletters and meetings and sometimes organize field trips, sports teams, writing clubs, book discussion groups—whatever appeals to the families involved. In general, it is not wise to start by asking your local school officials what the home-schooling law is—often they don't know, and they may give you misleading information.

2) DEVELOP YOUR CURRICULUM.

I need to emphasize that you don't need a packaged curriculum in order to homeschool successfully. You can write your own curriculum and change or adapt it as needed throughout the year and not run afoul with educational authorities. Many private schools have vastly different curricula from public schools (for instance, in schools using the educational philosophy of Rudolf Steiner, usually called Waldorf schools, children aren't taught to read until they've lost their eyeteeth, which is often later than when they would be taught in public school); many alternative schools use no set curricula at all! You can, too. Think of the resources available in your community: libraries, museums, historical sites, courthouses, specialty shops, nature centers. Think of adults you know who can share a skill, answer a question, let your children observe or help them at work. Think of real-life activities: writing letters, handling money, measuring, observing the stars, talking to older people. These are some of the ways that home-schoolers learn writing, math, science, and history. Talking with other homeschoolers will give you further ideas, as will reading the section on "Curriculum" (p. 33) and "Record Keeping" (p. 43).

Some families like to have an idea of what is expected of kids in school at various ages. You can ask a local schoolteacher, principal, or school board member for a copy of the curriculum outline for the grade your child would be in; some are happy to share this information, some are not. If you can get a copy of your school's curriculum, use it as a guide but don't make yourself follow it rigidly; one of the biggest advantages of homeschooling is that you don't have to operate exactly as school does or make your child follow the same timetable. Another useful document is the "Typical Course of Study, K-12" pamphlet, available for free from:

Worldbook International
4788 Highway 3775
Ft. Worth, TX 76116

You can call *Worldbook* and request your free copy as well: 800-967-5325.

For a more detailed, and unschooling-oriented curriculum guide, try Nancy Plent's *Living is Learning Curriculum Guides,* available from Holt Associates (p. 97). You can also use the *What Every First Grader Needs To Know* series edited by E.D. Hirsch to see what he thinks a "culturally literate" person needs to know at each grade level. Or ask your local Waldorf, Christian Independent, Montessori, Catholic, or other private school for their curriculum outlines.

Some families prefer to start out using a packaged curriculum. Appendix Two has the names of correspondence schools and curriculum supply houses, and you can investigate which one best fits your family's needs. You can also find ads for and reviews of curricula in many homeschooling magazines (pp. 96-98). Generally, a correspondence school's assignments can be completed in a few hours a day, leaving time for other activities.

There is no need to spend lots of money on curricula, books, educational toys and videos, etc. You really need to spend no more than you would ordinarily spend on a child's interests and activities. Homeschoolers often use the library and other free or low-cost community resources. They share or barter materials and skills with one another or with other people in the community. Some families are able to barter for outside lessons and to volunteer in exchange for admission to arts events or museums. Older homeschoolers find that volunteering is a good way to learn from adults outside the family, and it is often less expensive than taking a class or buying equipment.

3) Enjoy Your Family.

Don't let your family get lost in your efforts to school your children. It's easy to replace teachers, but not parents. Some parents burn out from homeschooling by trying to be demanding, "professional" teachers for some parts of the day, then sympathetic parents for other parts, and the stress of switching between these two roles becomes too burdensome. Be a parent to your children all the time. Teaching and helping our children learn is an inherent part of parenting that we seem to forget we do once we send children to school. We don't need to—though, perhaps, there are situations where one would want to—imitate classroom teacher behavior and techniques in homeschooling. If you want to take a break and walk through the woods because it is a gorgeous day, you can; the curriculum can wait. Perhaps something you discover in the woods will become a piece of your studies; perhaps it will just be a nice walk. If your child wants to finish an exciting book she is reading instead of doing lessons one day, you can permit that. The lessons can be caught up with later. Homeschooling lets us set our own goals and our own schedules. Don't let curricula and schooling become the tail that wags the dog in your home; enjoy your time together as a family.

Also, try not to compare yourselves too much with other homeschooling families; each is different. Some families, particularly in rural areas, have a slower pace of life and fewer opportunities for museum trips, specialized classes, and so on. They are able to take advantage of their land, homes, and nature in general in ways urban homeschoolers cannot. Further, some urban homeschoolers may prefer a slower pace of life than their colleagues who lead very active lives; being a homeschooler does not mean you must be plugged into every activity you can find.

CURRICULUM

Homeschooling changes and adapts to the needs of the learner, as well as to any special circumstances that may happen in the family (illness, a new baby, new job hours for a spouse, etc.). You do not, no matter what the law is in your state, need to plan out in precise detail what you will do for the entire year. However, you will probably want to have some sort of plan, or list of ideas, at the start.

What will we do in our homeschool?

It is useful for you and your spouse to clarify how you will homeschool, not only to answer skeptics' questions about what it is you're doing but also to keep yourselves from becoming rattled when things aren't going smoothly. It is also good to know where you stand philosophically so that you can present your homeschool in the best possible light to school officials who may question your approach. At the same time, it's crucial to remember that homeschooling is flexible. The word "homeschooling" doesn't refer to any one practice; it just refers to families learning outside of school. Choices you make at the start of the year are not irrevocable. You can—and you very likely will—adapt and change things as you go. You will also have many opportunities to learn from your mistakes, as we have found out in our own homeschooling. Live and learn!

All the books mentioned in this book will provide information, sometimes in great detail, as to the various methods of teaching and learning you may choose. For the sake of brevity, I will divide these approaches into two main philosophies:

1) School At Home

Families that choose this philosophy usually aren't worried about "why" their children must learn certain things at certain ages; they are far more concerned with how to make their children learn what they've decided their children should learn. Families with this philosophy of education have a large number of standardized textbooks and curricula to choose from and they typically can purchase them from school supply stores or textbook manufacturers. Often these materials can be purchased in used book stores, at homeschooling "curriculum fairs," and through direct mail. The curriculum determines what and when subjects will be taught, the parent creates or purchases lesson plans to use on the specified days, and the children are regularly tested to see how much of the material they have learned.

A subset of this category is often called the "unit study," "thematic," or "project" approach. Parents following this approach design a series of projects, field trips, and readings that build on a particular theme and use it to address several subject areas at once. For instance, one can use Thanksgiving time to study the Pilgrim era for history, biology (what food Pilgrims grew), science (how Pilgrims took care of illnesses), math (calculating how big a plot each person could get at Plymouth Plantation), etc. All in all, practitioners of this philosophy are taking the assumptions of conventional education and applying them to the smaller classroom they create in their homes.

2) UNSCHOOLING

This is also known as interest driven, child-led, natural, organic, or self-directed learning. John Holt coined the term in the late seventies to describe what we now call homeschooling. He disliked the "school at home" connotations of the word homeschooling and sought to find a better description, hence, "unschooling." When Holt coined the term he just wanted to use it as a more descriptive word than "homeschooling," as much learning takes place in the community and other places outside the home, while little of the learning happens in a traditional school way. Lately, the term "unschooling" has come to be associated with the type of homeschooling that doesn't use a fixed curriculum. When pressed, I define unschooling as allowing children as much freedom to learn in the world as parents are comfortable with. The advantage of this method is that it doesn't require you, the parent, to become someone else, i.e. a professional teacher pouring knowledge into child-vessels on a planned basis. Instead you live and learn together, with one interest leading to another. This is the way we learn before going to school and the way we learn when we leave school and enter the world of work. So, for instance, a young child's interest in hot rods can lead him to a study of how the engine works (science), how and when the car was built (history and business), who built and designed the car (biography), etc. Certainly these interests can lead to reading texts, taking courses, or doing projects, but the important difference is that these activities were chosen and engaged in freely by the learner. They were not dictated to the learner through curricular mandate to be done at a specific time and place. Unschooling, for lack of a better term (until people start to accept "living" as part and parcel of learning), is the natural way to learn. However, this does not mean unschoolers do not take traditional classes or use curricular materials when the student, or parents and children together, decide that this is how they want to do it. What it means is that unschoolers use these learning tools when they deem it makes sense to them to do so, not because they have reached a certain age or are compelled to do so by arbitrary authority. Therefore it isn't unusual to find unschoolers who are barely eight years old studying astronomy or who are ten years old and just learning to read.

It is unfair to think that either of the philosophies I present above are mutually exclusive of each other, though to some "school at homers" allowing children to determine what they will study is as distasteful as being forced to diagram sentences can be for some "unschoolers." Try not to let purists of either persuasion get to you. You must do what you are comfortable with; like your children, you, too, will learn and change as you get more experience with homeschooling. You can start out with a package of textbook and "teacher-proof curricula" (Honest! that's how some curriculum manufacturers refer to their materials) and if that isn't working you can switch to a unit study or unschooling approach. Indeed, you can do a little of each depending on your child's abilities and your ability to juggle different approaches. You may start out highly programmed and gradually loosen up and let your children have more say in what and how they study as you get comfortable with homeschooling. You may start out highly free-form and eventually find your child engaged in a very strict schedule of music lessons, Scout activities, and clubs. Indeed, I've heard more than one unschooler claim that what they actually do is "car-schooling," since that is where they spend so much of their time with their children while transporting them from one activity to another!

For in-depth descriptions of how learning and teaching occur in the course of growing older together, not primarily through planned lessons, read Nancy Wallace's book *Child's Work* to see how her childrens' free play eventually led them into rigorous music and composition classes. Micki and David Colfax's books *Homeschooling For Excellence,* and in particular, *Hard Times In Paradise* (both available from Mountain View Press, Box 246, Redwood Ridge Rd, Boonville, CA 95415) describe how their boys learned enough to get them into Ivy League schools by spending much of their youth developing and maintaining their rural family homestead.

A recent book by David Albert, *And The Skylark Sings With Me: Adventures in Homeschooling and Community-based Education,* describes how young children (the book ends with his oldest at age ten) spur adult learning as well as how parents can help children learn without always teaching them. It is particularly strong in science and nature education, both areas the parents knew nothing about until their children started asking questions.

You can also involve your children in creating their course of study for the year. Susan Jaffer of Pennsylvania wrote:

> ...Last year, at the beginning of the summer, I asked my daughters what I thought was a casual question: "What would you like to learn about this summer?" They began answering me right away, without so much as a pause, and this is what we ended up with: Suzanne, 8, wanted to learn about stories, poems, science, math, art, music, books, people, planting, animals, places, food, colors, rocks, babies, cars, eyes, and electricity. Gillian, 6, wanted to learn about seeds, bones, plants, books, evolution, dinosaurs, and experiments. I tend to think that the fact that I asked them in the summer freed them from the boundaries of school subjects. In any case, I was stunned by the fact that

they had so many subjects in mind, and that
their lists were right there waiting for me to ask
the right question...

I like Susan's phrase about how her kids expressed such wide interests since they were "freed... from the boundaries of school subjects." It reminded me of a comment I heard author Grace Llewellyn make about helping homeschooled teenagers find ways to study subjects outside of school by not always limiting ourselves to school subjects. Grace described a letter in *GWS* from a girl who asked what a person who studied whales was called. Her father told her such people were called "marine biologists." Grace pointed out that marine biology is but one way for children and adults to study and work with whales; the family could also encourage their daughter to study whales as an artist, musician, sailor, ecologist, naturalist, etc. This point is very valuable to remember if you find your child getting frustrated in their studies and you need a new way to approach the material.

Oddly enough, parents who follow alternative education ideas sometimes find that their children desire and flourish using conventional curricula. One fourteen-year-old girl strongly desired to use a packaged curriculum program to homeschool. This rattled her mom, an experienced unschooler, who had not used curricula with any of her children. They agreed to try homeschooling with a packaged curriculum, and the girl flourished with it.

A mother from Kentucky, Cindy Gaddis, sums up this issue quite well. She writes:

> I declare myself an unschooler even
> though my daughter Abbey loves workbooks

and my son Adam has to be taught most things in a highly structured manner. I say this because I am respecting their need to learn in the way that works best for them. I would declare an older homeschooler who decides to become much more structured in learning an unschooler because she is respecting her ability to know what she needs and wants at each stage of her life.

SCHEDULING

It is not unusual to feel overwhelmed by the amount of freedom learning at home allows, especially by those who were in school and are now being homeschooled. It often makes sense to let children get used to their new-found freedom gradually, allowing them more private time and space than they probably had before. But, as Susannah Sheffer writes:

> ...at some point the need for that break diminishes and kids begin to feel ready for more activity and focus, [and] it can be difficult to know where to start.
>
> One thing I've found useful, when helping kids go through this process, is to make three lists. One list is for things that come easily, things that you would do anyway, whether or not you sat down and made a plan about them. The second list is for things that you want to work on but feel you need some help with— maybe suggestions of ways to pursue the activity, or maybe some sort of schedule or plan regarding it. The third list is for things you

want to put aside for a while, things you don't want to work on right now.

The value of these lists, it seems to me, is that they show kids: (1) that they are already doing worthwhile things, and don't need outside intervention for everything; (2) at the same time, it's perfectly OK to want help in some areas, to have a list of things that you want to do but aren't sure what to do, and (3) that it's also OK to put some things aside for the time being. This might be especially important to kids who had bad experiences with particular subjects in school and who would benefit from realizing that they have much more control in their new situation. Fourteen-year-old Marianne was very emphatic, for example, about putting essay writing on list three, because she had had very unpleasant and discouraging experiences with essay writing in school, and for her, at that time, having control meant being able to say, "I choose not to work on that right now."

Marianne's list two was the longest, as I think it will be for many kids, and ultimately this list may be the most important, because it's the one from which ideas and plans can grow. As I said, it's very important to realize that much of what you're doing already has educational value (since school doesn't usually give kids credit for the things they willingly and eagerly pursue on their own). But it's just as important for the new homeschooler (or the long-time homeschooler who is looking to make some changes) to realize that it's fine to need help and to ask for it. Suppose a teenager has a vague feeling that she wants to do something with animals, but isn't sure what. That could go on list two. Then, when the lists are made up and you sit down to give each item closer attention, you can begin to think: what kind of work with animals? what kind of help would you need in making that happen? and so on.

The same goes for more traditional academic work. Suppose the homeschooler says, "I want to keep up with the other kids who are doing algebra in school, but I'm just not sure I'm going to do that regularly on my own." Well, that's OK. What would help? Should we look into finding another adult to work with you? Would it be fun to meet regularly with another homeschooler who is working on algebra? Or would a schedule tacked up to the bulletin board help you remember that you wanted to work on this each week?

Sometime people emphasize the lack of scheduling and fixed appointments in homeschooling, because this open-endedness is one of the things that makes homeschooling feel so different to kids who have spent years in school—no bells ringing, no one telling you you have to do math at this time. And it's true that we often want to stress the way in which homeschooling lets kids take advantage of whatever arises... But in stressing these benefits and these ways in which homeschooling is different from school, we may sometimes forget that the most crucial benefit, and difference, is that in homeschooling you have control—which means that you can make schedules, and plans, and appointments, if you want to.

In other issues of *GWS* we have stories by teens and elementary school-age children about the types of schedules and help they find useful. There are also many examples of how different families schedule their homeschooling in the firsthand accounts that are available in homeschooling periodicals and books.

Each family is different and each child is different, so don't assume that what worked for one child will work for them all. The most important thing, besides love, that you can bring to your homeschool is trust in yourself to help your children learn and trust in them to learn in their own way.

But I Can't Teach That!

You don't have to. Many homeschoolers find materials and good texts that the students can use to learn on their own, in addition to finding them tutors. These may be professional teachers, but are more likely to be people who are practitioners of what the child wishes to learn. This often puts parents in a different teaching role from that which occurs in schools; they are more facilitators, "askers," travel agents, general contractors, and counselors than instructors doling out lessons. Parents of homeschoolers learn to ferret out learning opportunities for their children, and they can become quite adept at networking through their local support groups, the Yellow Pages, local newspapers, and community bulletin boards. Sometimes they are instructors, no doubt. But the point is that parents do not have to be the sole instructors of their children.

Some homeschooling parents create clubs around certain interests their children may have, such as science, rocketry, magic, or theater, and conduct weekly meetings at their homes or in local libraries. Some share their expertise in exchange for money, barter, or no payment at all: a single mother we know charges families a modest fee for tutoring children in math at her home; another mother offers a free literature class in her home twice a week to ten homeschoolers; both mothers are former school teachers, by the way! This year a father we know who makes his living as an illustrator is teaching an art course once a week in the evening at his apartment, as a way to share his love of art with his sons and their friends. Ordinary people, using their own resources, can be highly effective teachers when they share their own interests with children who wish to learn from them.

Some homeschoolers create resource centers to be used by large numbers of homeschoolers, often forming alliances with local libraries for space and materials. In London, England, Leslie Barson created "The Otherwise Club" in her home as a place for children to work together on projects of their own choosing. As her children got older and the club got bigger Barson wanted to reclaim her home. She found a local community center that let her group meet two days a week for two thousand pounds a year; Barson charges a membership fee of one hundred pounds per family, and has been able to gain charitable status for the group. She writes:

> The Club provides the space for workshops and activities for families. We have three regular workshops—drama, pottery, and a science group for younger children—and we run a number of other activities. Past workshops have

included country dancing, visits from police dogs and their handlers, and talks by various experts in areas such as math, home education, and health. Recent workshops have included African drumming at several different levels and a workshop on *A Midsummer Night's Dream* and a trip to see the play.... The Otherwise Club has a small cafe which serves a vegetarian homemade lunch and cake as well as tea and coffee. This provides a small amount of funds and serves as a focal point for the community. We also keep a small lending library about alternative education and a large amount of information about activities and exhibitions in London...

Other homeschoolers find and publicize courses and offerings at local museums, historic sites, community centers, and gymnasiums. In Boston, Harvard University's Peabody Museum and the Boston Museum of Science advertise courses for homeschoolers. Technological advances now allow internet courses for learning everything from jazz improvisation to secondary school courses leading to diplomas; there are also video and audiotape lectures by experts in all kinds of fields that can be borrowed from libraries, or from homeschoolers who share the cost and the materials.

Most homeschooling, and certainly the formation and continuation of these clubs and groups, is performed by people not certified by the state as teachers, nor are their activities considered to be mandatory or graded. The participants get what they put into each activity, and should they decide not to learn in these settings, there is no external failing grade or other penalty for them. They can come back to these places and learn what they need when they are ready for it, or they can choose, or create, other situations in which they can learn what they wish to learn. These parents and children are not therefore recreating compulsory public school in their communities, nor are they creating alternative schools; they are creating alternatives *to* school for their children.

I hasten to add that some children need alternatives to home as well; clearly not every family is motivated to work with their children the way the homeschoolers I describe here are. However, the only place besides home for most children is school, a situation we have created with our compulsory education laws, and often school is not a good place for these children either. When neither home nor school is a safe, productive spot for children and teens to be, the sorts of third places that I describe above can be expanded to accommodate them. I doubt we can get people to change compulsory education laws in America, but there is wriggle-room in these laws, as homeschooling and many out-of-school programs sanctioned by various school departments demonstrate. By expanding these exceptions to allow children and teenagers to engage in and observe real work we will help them learn what is needed to do work well by watching or apprenticing with adults who share their interests. They also learn how to interact with others to get jobs done, and how to leave work they don't enjoy and find work they want to try; these are skills that are not only not taught in school, but actually tend to atrophy in most schools. One typically works in silence in competition for grades and is penalized for sharing information, and one can not change jobs when it is apparent that one does not have the capacity or interest to continue with a particular course in school and would like to try something different.

Not all things are apparently educational but that does not mean they are not important learning experiences for children. Play is, to me and many homeschoolers, a child's work. Children typically use fantasy play, in particular, not to escape from the real world, but to get into it: when they pretend to be doctors, fire-fighters, police, and soldiers, they are using their imaginations to explore these roles. My own children often played school when they were younger! People benefit from periods of play throughout life, and some people are able to find or create adult work that often grows out of their childhood play. School is all too often opposed to the play of children, a trend that is increasing as schools march to the drums of testing and standardization. *The London Times* published an article recently about research done by Dr. Jacqui Cousins, an adviser to the United Nations on early education, that shows four-year-olds in nursery schools feel upset and anxious about expectations for them to succeed at school. Some spoke seriously about not getting a job if they didn't work hard enough. One girl said that she had to work hard and not play so she could "get ready to pass my Key Stage One tests" (the tests given to five to seven-year-olds).

Homeschoolers need not turn the screws tighter on children in order to make them learn; there is no need to duplicate school techniques in our homes. However, there is often a perceived need, a worry by parents, and this worry touches all types of parents whether they are homeschooling or not, that they have to make their kids "buckle down and do some real learning." I hope that so far you have seen that there are many other ways and schedules to help your children learn besides those so often used in school.

RECORD KEEPING

There are two types of record keeping homeschoolers can do: that which is required by the state, and that which they want to do for themselves. Of course, there is some overlap, but on the whole these can be very different types of records. States, and in some cases local school districts, vary in the amount and the kind of recordkeeping they require of homeschoolers. The first thing you want to do is find out what you have to do legally (see page 29 for suggestions on how to do this). Some states require testing (but not always every year), some allow parents to choose among testing, keeping a portfolio, or writing up reports, and some states don't require recordkeeping at all. No matter what your state's requirements, you can find a way to fulfill them without getting bogged down or worrying more than is necessary about how much your children are accomplishing. In any case, whether or not your state has recordkeeping requirements, you may find, as many parents do, that you want to keep some kind of record of your homeschooling, for your own peace of mind and for the fun of chronicling your child's growth—just as parents have always saved their children's drawings, stories, projects, and so on.

Katharine Houk, a long-time homeschooler from New York, tells several ways to keep records:

> A topic that frequently comes up at homeschooling support group meetings at the beginning of the home school year is record keeping. For those of us whose homeschooling approach is interest-initiated and far-ranging, it can be a challenge to write quarterly reports

for submission to the school district, when learning is expected to be pigeonholed into subject areas.

When our family first started homeschooling, the New York State Home Instruction Regulation was not in effect. Homeschooling was permitted, but was handled differently by each school district, with guidelines from the State Education Department offering suggestions on how to handle homeschooling. Our district gave us a checklist to fill out periodically, and that was the extent of our reporting. But at that time, I kept daily logs of my children's activities, even though I didn't need them for reporting purposes. I was fascinated with their learning processes, and had great fun documenting all the wonderful things they did. Most of their learning was through play; they played intensely, happily, and for hours and days at a time. My challenge was in translating their activities and our conversations and experiences into a form that would fit in the subject area boxes in my log book.

When the need for reporting came along, with the passage of the current regulation, it was easy for us to make that transition; we had already been keeping records. Besides the requirement that as homeschoolers you must keep an attendance record (!), there is no specific requirement for record keeping in the regulation. But I knew that having a written record of our activities would be helpful to me in writing reports. Besides, I was already in the habit of doing it, and enjoyed creating a record of my children's learning.

I used a loose leaf notebook for each child.

In the front were pages that looked like a lesson plan book, with subject areas listed down the left side of the page, and the days of the week across the top of the page. I included Saturday and Sunday, because learning doesn't stop for weekends. In the notebook I also included a place to record field trips and keep photographs, pocket pages for papers, etc. It served us well, and the children enjoy looking back at them, laughing at the spelling in their early writings, and reminiscing about trips and other activities from years ago.

As the children grew older, I grew weary of sifting their learning into subject area categories. Their learning is all of a piece, and it became tedious to chop it up into artificial compartments on a daily basis. Therefore I changed the notebook to include lined paper, where each day I would write a few sentences about what was done that day. At the end of each month I would make a synopsis of the month by subject area. Then when it came time for a quarterly report I would have something to work from.

Now that the children are so much older (12 & 15), it is unnecessary for me alone to do all the record keeping. Also, my offspring are such independent learners and I am so busy that often I am not aware of their activities or of what books they are reading. I do jot things down from time to time that I am aware of and that I find especially noteworthy, but I ask each of them to keep their own notebook, and to write down the books they are reading and their activities, plus whatever else they care to put in their journals. This way I am not invading their privacy, and they have a record in their own writing of what they have done. At report time, they share with us the parts of their journals that they want in their reports. Privacy is an important issue, one that is sometimes not taken into account when school districts want to know everything that is happening with our children.

Some families I know use a spiral bound notebook for record keeping, and store papers in a separate portfolio. Also there are commercially distributed record-keeping systems you can purchase:

Night Owl Press markets a book called *Plan-It* that was intended for teachers in schools, but could be used by homeschoolers. For information, contact Richard Glaubman, Night Owl Press, 819 Cass St., Port Townsend, WA 98368.

A system created, especially for homeschoolers is the *Home Schoolers Journal,* available from FERG N US Services, PO Box 350, Richville, NY 13681; 315-287-9131.

For those of you who, with the proliferation of home computers, no longer use paper and pencil, there is a computer program especially for keeping track of your homeschooling. It is called The *Home School Organizer Made Easy* (HOME), and was created by a parent of five homeschoolers. The program is for IBM (and compatible) machines. For information contact Mary Roberson, Diligent Software, PO Box 750716, Memphis, TN 38175-0716.

Whatever method of record keeping you choose, the results will help you in writing reports and complying with assessment

requirements, and will be a wonderful chroni-
cle of your children's growth and development.

In about 14 states, as of this writing, homeschoolers must
formally write up their curriculum and submit it to their local
education authorities. In other states, requirements are less
extensive, so be sure to check the homeschooling laws or regulations in your state (see p. 29). For those states that do
require you to submit a curriculum or plan, here are some
guidelines.

If you purchase a curriculum, that is what you submit. You
transfer the program's stated goals and objectives onto whatever forms or documents the local education authorities wish
you to submit to them. If you follow your child's interests, as
I'm suggesting throughout this book, then it is largely a matter of translating what one is going to do anyway into language
the school officials can understand. We often print examples
of this "verbal judo" for dealing with this issue in *Growing
Without Schooling;* here is one for you to consider, prefaced by
editorial comment by Susannah Sheffer:

> ...In states that require written proposals in
> the first place (and not all do), the actual word-
> ing of the law, the requirements or preferences
> of the particular school district, and the incli-
> nations of the family itself will all influence
> what kind of proposal the family actually writes.
> Some people believe it's better to write a great
> deal so that the files are thick and the family
> appears thorough; others believe it's better to
> give only the minimum required by law and to
> let the school officials ask for more if they want
> more. Both approaches are valid. Some fami-

lies see the fact that they must write a proposal as an opportunity to articulate their own philosophy and goals for the year for themselves as well as for the district; others view the proposal only as something they must do to satisfy legal requirements and would rather keep it as short as possible. Again, both approaches are valid... Here's a sample of an effective, shorter proposal [for 1st grade—PF] that Jane Dwinell (Vermont) wrote for her daughter Dana's first year of homeschooling (again, in the legal sense):

Course of Study for Dana Dwinell-Yardley:

1. Basic Communication Skills—Language Arts

Topics may include but shall not be limited to the following: Silent and oral reading; listening skills; telling stories; spelling; homonyms; synonyms and antonyms; writing letters, stories, and poems by hand, dictation, or typing; dictionary use for meaning and spelling; encyclopedia use; library skills, use of basic punctuation; use of table of contents and index; and computer skills.

Basic Communication Skills—Math

Topics may include but shall not be limited to the following: Count and write by 1s, 10s, 100s, 1000s; addition and subtraction with single and double digits; telling time and using the calendar; value of coins and making change; and meaning of inch, foot, yard.

2. Citizenship, History, and Government in Vermont and the U.S.

Topics may include but shall not be limited to the following: Current events; Town

Meeting; travel throughout New England and to Florida; national holidays; map reading: World—name and find oceans, continents, our country, our state; U.S.—name and find New England states; VT—find Irasburg, Montpelier, Burlington, Newport, Lake Memphremagog, Lake Champlain, Lake Willoughby, Lake Morey, Connecticut River, Black River, Barton River.

3. Physical Education and Comprehensive Health Education
Topics may include but shall not be limited to the following:

Sports—cross country skiing, downhill skiing, sliding, biking, hiking, tree climbing, swimming, gymnastics, badminton, croquet, canoeing. Health Education - basic first aid for cuts, splinters, burns, sprains and strains; treatment of common cold; care of teeth and regular dental visits; traffic safety; family meal planning and food preparation.

4. English, American, and Other Literature
Topics may include but shall not be limited to the following: Novels by 19th and 20th century British and American authors; American poetry; Greek mythology.

5. The Natural Sciences
Topics may include but shall not be limited to the following: Seeds, bulbs, plants and flowers; common birds; sun, moon, stars and basic constellations; seasons, weather, clouds; fire and temperature; farm animals—care from infancy to adulthood, slaughtering; maple sugaring.

6. The Fine Arts

Topics may include but shall not be limited to the following: Drawing; painting; computer graphics; making clothes and handkerchiefs for dolls and dress-up; attending concerts and plays; listening to music at home (live and taped); singing.

Further Resources For Thinking About and Planning Your Homeschooling Year (see also pp. 15–16; 107–123):

The Art of Education: Reclaiming Your Family, Community, and Self, Linda Dobson

Awakening Your Child's Natural Genius, Thomas Armstrong

Budgetext Used Textbook Catalog, Toll free: 888-888-2272

Countdown to Consistency, Mary Hood (PO Box 2524, Cartersville GA 30120)

Homeschooling On A Shoestring, M. Morgan and J. Alee

How Children Learn, John Holt

How Children Fail, John Holt

I Learn Better By Teaching Myself/Still Teaching Ourselves, Agnes Leistico

In Their Own Way, Thomas Armstrong

Learning All the Time, John Holt

Teach Your Own: A Hopeful Path for Education, John Holt

EVALUATION

John Holt wrote at length about marking and grading in his book *What Do I Do Monday?* Here is an excerpt to give you some context about evaluations outside of conventional schooling:

> In the kind of learning I have been talking about there is no place and no need for conventional testing and grading. In a class where children are doing things, and not getting ready to do them sometime in the distant future, what they do tells us what they have learned.
>
> …What sense does an average grade make in a course like English? Do we average a serious writer's best work against his worst? If I assigned a paper, and a student did badly on it, this only showed that this was the wrong paper for him, where he could not show the ability he had. The remedy was to try and give a wide enough variety of choices and opportunities for writing, reading, and talking so that everyone would have a fairly good chance of showing his best talents.
>
> It is not just in English that it makes no sense to figure students' grades by taking an average of all their daily or weekly work. It makes no sense in any subject…
>
> …It is not grading alone that is stupid, but the whole idea of trying to have a class move along on a schedule, like a train. Children do not learn things at the same time, or equally easily and quickly.

Nonetheless, many states require homeschoolers to provide a form of evaluation during, or at the end of, the school year. Some states require standardized tests, others provide several evaluation options, and some states require no evaluations at all. You should determine what your state's requirements are for this before settling on an evaluation procedure (see p. 29). Homeschoolers can typically choose from the following evaluation methods:

STANDARDIZED TESTING. This can be provided by the school, or, in some cases, you can negotiate to use a third party, such as a guidance counselor, teacher, or mutually agreed upon proctor, to administer the test in your home. If you feel the school's choice of test is biased against your homeschooling methods and philosophy, you can ask to administer a different test more to your liking. Before doing this, it is wise to consider how and what you will be teaching your children; if you are following a school curriculum and periodically giving your children tests, then they are probably ready to take these standardized tests. If you have created an individualized study plan for your child, and you do not use standardized testing during your homeschooling year, but your school is forcing standardized tests on you, then it is wise to do as they do in school: get a hold of previous editions of the test, spend some time teaching the subject matter that you see is on the test, and practice taking the test with your children.

PORTFOLIO ASSESSMENTS. This, combined with a yearly progress report, is how my wife and I handle evaluations of our children for our local district. A portfolio is an extension of the refrigerator magnet: a place where you save and date your children's work. The difference is you want to save a lot of this stuff and sift through it later to find significant pieces of achievement or indications of development for school officials, such as the two page report on "the real Pocahontas" our daughter Lauren (then 9) did, or problem solving, such as a series of math problems, with her self-corrections, that Alison (then 6) did. We also save workbook pages (our children sometimes ask for workbook pages just to see if they can do the same stuff their schooled friends do!), lists of books we buy or check out from the library to read to them or that they read themselves, and brief journal notes about significant events, such as a trip to Plymouth Plantation when Lauren and a friend helped bake bread and make candles "the real way" by spending all day in one "Pilgrim's" house.

PROGRESS REPORTS. These can take the form of written narratives of your children's learning over a quarter, a half-year, or a year; the periodicity of these reports will depend on your state laws or regulations. Consider that if you write at least one sentence a day, or at least five sentences at the end of each week, about each child, by the end of the year you will have many pages of detailed information about what your children actually did, rather than just a letter or number for a year's worth of work.

PERFORMANCE ASSESSMENTS. This term refers to the evaluation of the culmination of a body of work. These are becoming more in vogue with current education reforms. For example, a child could successfully build a working volcano to demonstrate mastery of certain science principles, or actually perform in a play or concert. Many real-life activities demonstrate thought, responsibility, planning and subject mastery. For example, a child might, for the ultimate purpose of setting up an aquarium, determine how much money he has, budget it properly, and choose the right fish and equipment. This particular example is taken from literature by the Wisconsin Department of Education about how it plans to evaluate students as part of education reforms.

Assessments can also take the form of interviews with other types of educators (child psychologists; school counselors, etc.), written reports from people other than relatives and parents who work with your child, and videotapes, audio tapes, and newspaper clippings of activities your children do that prove they can use the skills and knowledge they have learned.

HOMESCHOOLERS, COLLEGE, AND WORK

Many homeschoolers have been admitted to college or found work worth doing without college degrees. Researchers have studied grown homeschoolers and found them to be doing well individually and economically (see Appendix 1 as well). However, talking to these former homeschoolers who make themselves available to others by speaking at conferences, writing books, or listing themselves in *GWS's* "Grown Homeschoolers" can give you a clearer and more complete sense of how homeschooling has served them.

In general, homeschoolers apply to college just like anyone else, except they need to prepare their own transcripts or simply summarize what they have been doing, and be sure they have covered the subject matter that each college requires of first-year students. Cafi Cohen's book, *And What About College? How homeschooling leads to admissions to the best colleges and universities,* not only details her children's successful college application process, but covers all aspects of applying to college, including financial aid issues, applying to a military service academy, how to create high school transcripts, etc.

Two popular books by Micki and David Colfax, *Homeschooling For Excellence* and *Hard Times In Paradise* (see p. 38 for ordering information), describe how they homeschooled their children, and how they handled college admissions (three of their boys graduated Harvard).

Further, home-based education programs run by private schools, such as the Clonlara School and others, (p. 77–80), will provide high school degrees and transcripts for colleges. There are other types of homeschooling programs for teenagers as well. They are oriented toward internship and apprenticeship opportunities rather than conventional school work (see p. 115, "Opportunities, Activities").

All homeschooling periodicals (see p. 50 for some) print stories about how homeschoolers get into college or find interesting work without college degrees. Many famous people who were homeschooled or who never graduated or attended college have made important contributions to society, such as: Susan B. Anthony, Pearl Buck, Andrew Carnegie, Thomas Edison, Winston Churchill, Charles Dickens, Michael Faraday, Benjamin Franklin, Jane Goodall, Alex Haley, Patrick Henry, Eric Hoffer, Claude Monet, Gen. George Patton, Bertram Russel, Woodrow Wilson, Gloria Stienem, Mark Twain, and the Wright Brothers. Attending school is not the only way for people to become valuable members of society and contributors to our culture.

I hope you see how homeschooling can be inherently different from traditional schooling. Once you start investigating resources (which make up the rest of this book), talking with your children about learning, and meeting other homeschoolers, you will find for yourself how one subject naturally leads to another and you will discover that you have, indeed, created a "curriculum" for yourself about how to be a homeschool parent. The most important thing to do now is to do it! Enjoy your time with your children and the rest will follow.

Further Resources For Thinking About and Planning For Going From Homeschool to College and Work

An "A" In Life: Famous Homeschoolers, Mac and Nancy Plent
Bear's Guide To Earning College Degrees Nontraditionally, Dr. John Bear
Ferguson's Career Resources Catalog, Ferguson Publishing Company, 200 West Jackson Blvd, Chicago, IL 60606
Occupational Outlook Handbook, US Department of Labor. Available on-line at: www.bls.gov/ocohome.htm
Peterson's Guide to Independent Study, Peterson's Guide

SOME SELECTIVE COLLEGES THAT HAVE ADMITTED HOMESCHOOLERS

Competitiveness ratings (based on *Barron's Profiles of American Colleges*) are: ***Most Competitive, **Highly Competitive, *Very Competitive.

*	Agnes Scott College, GA
***	Amherst College, MA
*	Austin College, TX
***	Boston College, MA
**	Boston University, MA
**	Brigham Young University, UT
**	Brown University, RI
***	CA Institute of Technology, CA
*	Calvin College, MI
**	Carleton College, MI
**	Carnegie-Mellon University, PA
*	Christendom College, VA
***	College of William and Mary, VA
***	Cornell University, NY
*	Covenant College, GA
***	Dartmouth College, NH
**	GMI Engineering and Management Institute, MI
*	Grand Valley State University, MI
**	Grove City College, PA
*	Harding University, AK
***	Harvard University, MA
***	Harvey Mudd College, CA
***	Haverford College, PA
*	Hillsdale College, MI
*	Houghton College, NY
*	John Brown University, AK
**	Kenyon College, OH
*	Loyola College, MD
***	Massachusetts Institute of Technology, MA
*	Messiah College, PAa
***	Middlebury College, VT
*	Mississippi State University, MS
***	Northwestern University, IL
*	Oakland University, MI
**	Oberlin College, OH
*	Oklahoma State University, OK
***	Oxford University, Great Britain
**	Pennsylvania State University, PA

*	Pepperdine University, CA
***	Princeton University, NJ
**	Rensselaer Polytechnic, NY
**	Rhodes College, TN
***	Rice University, TX
**	Rose-Hulman Institute of Technology, IN
*	State University of New York, Buffalo, NY
***	Swarthmore College, PA
*	Taylor University, IN
**	Thomas Aquinas College, CA
***	U. S. Air Force Academy, CO
***	U. S. Naval Academy, MD
*	Univ. of Alabama, Huntsville, AL
*	Univ of Colorado, Boulder, CO
**	Univ. of California, Berkeley, CA
**	Univ. of CA, Los Angeles, CA
*	Univ. of CA, Santa Cruz, CA
***	University of Chicago, IL
*	University of Dallas, TX
*	University of Evansville, IN
**	University of Michigan, MI
**	University of Minnesota, MN
*	Univ. of Missouri, Kansas City, MO
*	Univ. of Missouri, Rolla, MO
**	University of North Carolina, NC
***	University of Pennsylvania, PA
*	University of Texas, Austin, TX
***	University of Virginia, VA
*	University of Washington, WA
**	University of Wisconsin, WI
**	Vanderbilt University, TN
*	Virginia Wesleyan College, VA
**	Washington University Medical Center, MO
**	Wheaton College, IL
**	Whitworth College, WA
***	Williams College, MA
**	Worcester Polytechnic Institute, MA
***	Yale University, CT

— From *And What About College? How homeschooling leads to admissions to the best colleges and universities,* by Cafi Cohen

APPENDIX ONE

HOMESCHOOLING BEFORE 1977

As noted elsewhere, homeschooling is not a modern phenomenon and has been with us in various forms since humans inhabited the earth. In modern times we have come to equate education with schooling, but the two are hardly the same. Indeed, given society's penchant for "adding value" to merchandise by proclaiming the merchandise "educational" (for instance, computer games are now called "edutainment"), it is hard to imagine that education will refer only to schooling in the future. Looking at the past is a good way to put some firm "land" under our homeschooling feet.

It is also good to read books about homeschooling from other eras in order to see how questions got answered about how much structure should be used in one's homeschool, or when academics should be taught, and to see that there never was a "golden age" of schools where kids obeyed teachers, passed tests with flying colors, and loved school with a passion we have lost today. Perhaps such places exist in Garrison Keillor's Lake Wobegon, but never anywhere else.

Here are some references for reading about homeschooling in previous years. You can find these materials in used bookstores, the archives of college libraries, or, occasionally, through interlibrary loan. In particular, you might be interested in our collection *Growing Without Schooling: A Record of a*

Grassroots Movement, Vol. 1, Aug. 1977–Dec. 1979 to see how far our laws and perceptions of homeschooling have changed in the past two decades. Many of the writers in these early issues identified themselves only by their initials as they were afraid of reprisals from school officials. Homeschooling has come a long way since then, but as you will see, it has always been part of the fabric of twentieth century American education. Indeed, if you come across old encyclopedias, you can look up "Domestic Education" and read about how homeschooling was done years ago. The US Library Of Congress listed homeschooling books under this heading until the late 1980s.

The work of Charlotte Mason has been brought back into print and is popular with some modern homeschoolers. Mason was a nineteenth century British educator who wrote a series of books which advocated homeschooling as a way to nurture Christian values and mastery of subject matter. Her approach emphasizes the Bible and the traditional subject areas of a British prep school education, such as Latin. Her warm attitude and respect towards children and their learning is sensitive and ahead of its time.

For further reading: Charlotte Mason Research & Supply, Box 172, Stanton, NJ 08885.

For The Children's Sake, Susan Schaeffer Macauley

John Holt once wrote that he didn't think school was a good idea gone bad, but that the entire idea of putting kids into a room and forcing them to learn the same thing at the same time was nutty from the start. Here is some strong evidence that schooling was failing and in need of reform as far back as at least 1892. This book is particularly interesting not only because the author claims public schooling is a failure, but because he advocates homeschooling in its place. This is from *The School In the Home*, by Tufts University Professor A.A. Berle (Moffit Yard, NY, 1912):

"American education is one of the most wasteful things in the whole American organization of life... The evidence of this indictment of our public education can be had on the most casual inquiry. Ask any well-informed parent about his children's progress in school and you will get at once a cry of discontent and helpless protest. Such protests, in the shape of letters of inquiry about the subject-matter of this book, are in my possession by the hundreds. They come from all sorts of people, from college professors to the street laborers... The one thing about them all is, that they see with more or less clearness that the education on which we spend so much money and about which we boast so loudly and about which we are in such deadly earnest as communities and so indifferent as individuals, is a fearfully wasteful and costly process. And in nothing more costly than in the loss to the mental habits and personal intellectual ideals of young people themselves. We could possibly endure it if it did no good. But it does not stop there; it is demoralizing the mental habits of the nation...

"...Ask any teacher who has watched the progress of the public schools in the last twenty years. The teacher... will tell you in plain terms, that while the teachers are doing the best they can under the circumstances, the results are steadily more discouraging, if any high and thorough standard is taken into consideration. He will tell you that the capacity for steady and sustained thought on the part of pupils seems to grow less instead of more."

A volunteer at our office, Patrick Hanley, put this out-of-print book in my hands recently. Like some of the early home-schoolers who wrote to *GWS* in the late seventies, *A Mother's Letters To A Schoolmaster* (Alfred A. Knopf, NY, 1923) was written anonymously, though Mr. Hanley has identified her as Rita Sherman, of New York City. Currently, that is all we know about her biographically. Here is the complete table of contents of this remarkable book, followed by a few quotations:

TABLE OF CONTENTS

I   In which a little boy plays truant and why

II   In which it is plainly to be seen that democracy cannot be learned in a place where it is not lived

III   In which a little boy builds a school

IV   Which shows how to teach not by telling, but by doing Education by participation

VI   Wherein it is set forth that education should proceed upon an understanding of the everyday facts of life and living, and wherein a Chart of these is given so that even "he that runs may read"

VII   Which denies the assertion that adults are any better able to think than children, and avers that quality of thought is a more important consideration than quantity of know edge

VIII   "Finding out" along ways of pleasantness and paths of purpose

IX   In which is repudiated the shameful plea that the State need sacrifice any high educational ideal to a specious expediency

X   Wherein is related how a little boy learned to read while he was learning to talk

XI   Which makes plain that it only seems more natural for a child to talk than to read because he is not permitted to learn to do both together. There was a time when men did neither. The fact that visual symbols of words developed later than sound symbols of words does not make one more natural than the other.

XII   Wherein is shown how by guiding a child's natural inter ests, he enters into that heritage whereby he "begins to learn everything the moment he begins to learn anything"

XIII   Which foretells, briefly, how that which we build as an inspiring workshop for our children, may become a temple for ourselves

XIV   A Mother's Program of Public Education, wherein is shown how parents, teachers and citizens together may associate to initiate, build and maintain Children's Community Centres of Work, Play and Information, and how in an orderly manner, true education may happily obtain therein

From *In which a little boy plays truant and why*

"Dear Sir,

I have your letter saying that the Board of Education has agreed, in the case of my little boy, to what you call a "temporary suspension of the compulsory attendance laws."

... It occurred to me as I listened to you the other day that the great difference between us is that you think education begins and ends with the school, but I think education begins with the child and never ends.

No wonder, with this divergence, that we talked to each other in different tongues, that what to you is truancy, to me is simply freedom; that what to Peter is work, to you is idling; that what to Peter is play, to you is "dangerous cramming." It is not often that I need come in contact with views such as yours, and I might, under your strenuous self-assurance, have had some misgivings as to this free and happy course, had not Peter been along to cheer and champion me. I was altogether cleared however, of craven self-mistrust when, after you faced him with the ominous invitation: ""But don't *you* want to come to school, young man?" he answered, with a confidence equalling your own, and with a politeness which scarcely covered up his entire lack of enthusiasm for your proposal:

'No, sir, thank you! ...You see, *I'm so busy!*'"

From *In which it is plainly to be seen that democracy cannot be learned in a place where it is not lived:*

"Sir:

Your reply to my letter attempts to refute the charge that your schools do not stress the development of character needful to an understanding and practice of democratic citizenship. Stripped of the euphuism with which you defend your argument, what you uphold is simply the doctrine of authority by force.

...You are confusing self-restraint, which is a moral factor (the result of a deliberate choice between an expression of goodwill and one of evil), with self-repression, a characteristic fruit of fear or tyranny. There is no self-restraint, sir, without a present opportunity for *self-expression*. Where the free expression of thought is restricted by pressure, you smother enough good to outweigh a thousand times the evil you fear too much openly to grapple with. I think if children do develop character through this specious discipline of yours, it is not the character of which democracy is bred. Such discipline may make a child afraid to do wrong, but it will scarcely breed within him the desire to do good. It is by this desire, sir, and not by fear, that free men flourish.

...We, the State, have for a hundred years, gathered our children together in school, from all classes of society, upon a common ground, for a common purpose, and then have rested our case for a democratic education upon the self-satisfied assumption that this democracy of *intent* is sufficient, even final. We have allowed it to presuppose a democracy applied, practiced, and produced!

We must be rid of this vanity. An honest analysis will show you that the school as a democratic institution has progressed no farther than a decree of compulsory attendance."

From *Wherein is shown how by guiding a child's natural interests, he enters into that heritage whereby he "begins to learn everything the moment he begins to learn anything"*

"...Alongside these literary matters [she has described the plays, stories, and other writing Peter saves—PF], I find much information scribbled down about baseball—line-ups, score-cards and records galore of the glorious doings of his heroes of the diamond.

Someone, seeing this mass of material on Peter's shelves of the desk, said to me: "But when does he do his lessons? And what about discipline?"

Discipline—yes, and lessons, too,—grow out of the should itself when it is unfolding in joyous activity. Discipline comes from the need of harmoniously carrying through what one has begun, because it is so interesting (or, as Peter says, so *important*) to do it. Lessons are only valuable when they are things learned in the course of carrying out an idea.

To one who had not sensed from the beginning what the fruitage must inevitably be, it would indeed seem a far cry from such homely things as kisses, or such pastimes as base-ball, to arithmetic; or from license numbers to density of world population, agricultural conditions and the status of farm laborers; from a toy engine to governments; or from a safety-match to the lumber industry. But it is with just such matter-of-fact starting-points, connected with real life, that Peter (and why not any and every child?) has come happily along to the place to which most fourteen-year-old children crept "like a snail unwillingly."

"I should think it would make you nervous to have to clear up so much!" said the visitor I have just quoted.

It was plain to me that she objected to the temporary dis-arrangement of my living-room, to the toy-theatre under the table, and the breastworks Peter has left in the wicker chair he uses for a fort. I could only tell her of my own heartfelt wish that I could find a school-group in a children's building where my little boy, with many others, might play out his projects as freely as he could do in his own home. Failing to find such an environment for him elsewhere, what moral right have I to interfere with his ardent energy and creative vigor? Children are people, too."

I found the following in the Utah Home Education Association's June, 1995 newsletter (see p. 94). Below I quote Dr. Larry Arnoldson of Brigham Young University who wrote:

"I recently came upon a most interesting book, *The Home Education of a Boy* by William B. Barrett, published in 1950... the first three chapters were published earlier as three sepa-rate articles...Then in 1950 the three articles, plus two others, 'John Today' and 'If I Could Do It Over Again' were added to the earlier articles and all of them were published as a book...

"In reporting on Barrett's book I will mostly look at the final chapter which is titled, 'If I Could Do It Over Again'...

"First [Barrett] said, 'I would approach the problem of building self-confidence from a wholly different direction. John was painfully slow to learn in any field which was foreign to his natural instincts.'

"He says he had thought it was his duty to make his son

master his shortcomings. That, he felt, had been the wrong thing to do. He should have built upon his '...son's abilities, his natural tendencies, his strengths.'

"He said for example, '...if mathematics happened to be his poorest subject and history his best, I would try and build on history... constructively. I would analyze history against mathematics, and try to show what they had in common... I would approach the subject on a basis of interest, enthusiasm, confidence... discovery...' He would avoid, '...dread, impatience, worry, criticism, despair,... scolding, nagging, ...fear.'

"...A second insight Barrett received was, 'There is another part of John's education of which... I am not too proud: my overstressing of punctuality and orderliness. Not that these are unimportant, but that... I would try to "sell" John on their value rather than "policing" him, as I now realize I often did.'

"...A third lesson Barrett said he learned was, 'If I had it to do over again, I think I would bring up more of my own problems for discussion in the family circle, as an example to John, of the wisdom of being less secretive, and the value of getting the perspective of other minds on personal and family problems.'

"He says he would reveal himself as a person trying to live effectively in coping with the world. 'We should treat our youngsters much more adultly than it is natural for us to do...'

"...Another thing Barrett wouldn't do if he had it to do over again is, '...assume that all Television programs John was watching were a waste of time... I would avoid being superior about his Television tastes. Children hate parental superiority.

" '...What would I do? ... explore with him open mindedly. I would join him when he was watching TV. I would look for all the good points of acting, set design, camera work, etc. I would comment favorably on these On occasion I would note something poorly done. I might ask John from time to time what he thought about a particular aspect of a programs. In other words, I would encourage a critical and objective faculty in him...

" 'Additionally I would attempt to turn TV into a valuable educational tool... some story... might be looked up and read, a city might be located on a globe, a really good joke that might be told the family at dinner, anything that might suggest a game to play or something to make—I would try to interest my son in following it...)

" 'In short I believe Television can supply a great many educational opportunities if parents will stop bewailing and try with intelligence and enthusiasm to fit it into their program of home education.'

"My, my, was this said about television in the 1940's? TV was considered a bad thing clear back then? Barrett adds a note of caution in summary of the various lessons he claims to have learned up to this point. Children... 'should not be smothered with parental surveillance.'

"Barrett's final point, but undoubtedly not the least important to be made, is, 'If I were permitted to repeat the experience of educating my son, I would abandon the grown-up conception that child training is a one-way enterprise. I realize now that I learned as much, if not more than John, as I worked with him. Given the opportunity to repeat the experience, I would approach the process as one of self-education, as well as of training for my son.'"

Adults who were homeschooled shed some interesting light on other ways children can grow into successful adults without going through years of school. Guiomar Goransson-Martin wrote to *Growing Without Schooling* magazine in 1994:

"I'm 38 and I was homeschooled before it was called homeschooling… we traveled a great deal…

"The school officials were always calling, dropping by, and otherwise hassling my parents whenever we were back in Detroit. My parents went to countless meetings with the principals and agreed to have me tested to the school's satisfaction. I always tested above my grade level.

"…I was never pressured into reading. It was just something I evolved into, I suppose from being surrounded by books and seeing everyone in my family reading them. Also, I was read to constantly.

"…I was accepted at a local one-year college for secretarial studies. After that year I applied and was accepted into three different nursing programs…"

APPENDIX TWO

CORRESPONDENCE SCHOOLS OR CURRICULUM SUPPLIERS

A Beka Correspondence School/Home Video School/Book Publications, Pensacola FL 32523-9160; 1-800-874-BEKA

Alpha Omega Publications, PO Box 3153, Tempe AZ 85281; 602-438-2717

Alta Vista College Press Home School Curriculum, PO Box 222, Medina WA 98039; 206-453-7848

American Home Academy Materials, 2770 S 1000 W, Perry UT 84302

American School, 850 E 58th, Chicago IL 60637 (high school)

Associated Christian Schools, PO Box 27115, Indianapolis IN 46227; 317-881-7132

Brigham Young University-Dept. of Independent Study, 206 Harman Continuing Ed Bldg, Provo UT 84602

Calvert School, 105 Tuscany Rd, Baltimore MD 21210; 410-243-6030

Christian Liberty Academy, 502 W Euclid Ave, Arlington Hts IL 60004

Classic Curriculum, Dept. G, PO Box 656, Milford MI 48042; 313-481-7008 or 1-800-348-6688

Clonlara Home Based Education Program, see "Helpful Private Schools" below

Educators Publishing Service, 31 Smith Pl, Cambridge MA 02138; 617-547-6706

Glenn Distributors, 7251 Bass Hwy, St Cloud MN 32769

Hewitt Research Foundation, PO Box 9, Washougal WA 98671; 360-835-8708

Home Study Alternative School, PO Box 10356, Newport Beach CA 92658

Home Study Directory, National Home Study Council, 1601 18th St NW, Washington DC 20009

Home Study Int'l, 6940 Carroll Ave, Takoma Park MD 20912; 301-680-6000

International Institute, PO Box 99, Park Ridge IL 60068

Kolbe Academy, 1600 F St, Napa CA 94559

Laguna Beach Educational Books, 245 Grandview, Laguna Beach CA 92651; 714-494-4225

Laurel Spring School, PO Box 1440, Ojai 93024

The Learning Experience Company, PO Box 1457, Bryson City NC 28713; 800-367-8532

Living Heritage Academy, PO Box 1438, Lewisville TX 75067

McGuffey Academy, 2213 Spur Trail, Grapevine TX 76051; 817-481-7008

The Moore Foundation, Box 1, Camas WA 98607; 360-835-2736

National Book Company, 333 SW Park Ave, Portland OR 97205-3784; 503-228-6345

Oak Meadow School, PO Box 740, Putney VT 05346; 802-387-2021

Our Lady of Victory School, 4436 E Alpine Dr, Post Falls ID 83854; 208-773-7265

Phoenix Special Programs, 3132 W Clarendon, Phoenix AZ 85017 (high school)

Rod & Staff Publishers, Crockett KY 41413; 606-522-4348

School for Young Performers, 2472 Broadway Suite 312, New York NY 10025; 1-800-390-5899 (K-12; students can enroll for one course or the full program)

Seton School Home Study, 1 Kidd Ln, Front Royal VA 22630-3332; 540-636-9990

SMM Educational Services, Box 1079, Sunland CA 91040 818-352-2310

University of Nebraska Independent Study High School, Continuing Ed Ctr Rm 269, Lincoln NE 68583

Weaver Curriculum, 2752 Scarborough, Riverside CA 92503 (Pre K-6th, 7-12th supplements)

HELPFUL PRIVATE SCHOOLS

Private schools enrolling or helping homeschoolers in various ways (curricula, legal help, support).

Abbott Loop Christian Center, 2626 Abbott Rd, Anchorage AK 99507

Abbington Academy, Box 3303, Gibbs Av, Wareham MA

02571; 508-291-1229 (Cape Cod only)

Arivaca Community School, PO Box 24, Arivaca AZ 85601

Branford-Grove School, PO Box 341172, Arleta CA 91334; 818-890-0350

Bay Shore School, PO Box 13038, Long Beach CA 90803; 310-434-3940

Cascade Canyon School, 459-3464 (San Anselmo, CA)

Clonlara Home Based Education Program, 1289 Jewett St, Ann Arbor MI 48104; 734-769-4515

Cooperative Learning Center, 454 Papaya St, Vista CA 92083; 619-726-3020

Dayspring Christian Academy, PO Box 60956, Palo Alto CA 94306

G.A.T.E. School, 1725 N Date #43, Mesa AZ 85201

Grassroots Free School, 2458 Grassroots Way, Tallahassee FL 32301; 904-656-3629

HCL Boston School, PO Box 2920, Big Bear City CA 92314; 909-585-7188

Horizon Academy, 21102 Pleasant Park Rd, Conifer CO 80433; 303-697-8158

Independence Private School, c/o Principal: M. Black, 45 Albert St North, Orilla, ONT L3V 5K3, Canada

The Learning Community, 9085 Flamepool Way, Columbia MD 21045; 410-730-0073

The Learning Community, Inc, PO Box 5177, Herndon VA 22070

Little Piney School, Rt 1 Box 20, Newburg MO 65550

Little Red Home School, 9669 E 123rd, Hastings MN 55033; 437-3049

Magic Meadow School, PO Box 29, N San Juan CA 95960

Meter Schools, PO Box 427, Rosharon TX 77583

Mount Vernon Academy, 184 Vine St, Murray UT 84107

Mt. Carmel Academy, RD 1 Box 1737, Waterville VT 05492

Newbridge School, 3131 Olympic Blvd, Santa Monica CA 90404; 310-315-3056

Pilgrim Christian School, 3759 E 57th St, Maywood CA 90270; 213-585-3167

Pinewood School, 112 Road D, Pine CO 80470; 303-670-8180

Puget Sound Community School, 1715 112 Av NE, Bellevue WA 98004; 206-455-7617

Rocky Mountain High Academy, PO Box 418, Flora Vista NM 87415

Santa Fe Community School, PO Box 2241, Santa Fe NM 87501; 505-471-6928

Seedling, c/o Joy Reiter, 69 Sanderson Crescent, Richmond Hill Ontario L4C 5L5, Canada

Sidney Ledson School, 33 Overland Dr, Don Mills, Ont, Canada M3C 2C3; 416-447-5355

TEACH, 4350 Lakeland Ave, N Robbinsdale MN 55422

Thalassa!, 5917 Oak Av, Suite 176, Temple City CA 91780-2404; 818-287-8595

Upattinas School, 429 Greenridge Rd, Glenmoore PA 19343; 610-458-5138

The Venice Community School, 31191 Road 180, Visalia 93292; 209-592-4999

Virtual High and WonderTree Education Society, PO Box 380, Vancouver BC V5Z 4L9, Canada 604-739-5941

HOMESCHOOLING
ORGANIZATIONS

Some of these groups are statewide (look for the state name in the group's title as an indication) and are likely to have information about state laws or regulations, and may have conferences and packets of information for new homeschoolers. Other groups are local support groups that are likely to have meetings and activities. Both state and local groups may have newsletters. Try getting in touch with a state group even if it's far away from where you live; many state groups can refer you to families, or smaller support groups, in your immediate area.

STATE OR LOCAL GROUPS: (ALPHABETICALLY BY STATE)

AL: **East Lake UMC Academy,** 1603 Great Pine Rd, Birmingham 35235 (acts as cover school)

Valleydale Home School Academy, 2408 Valleydale Rd, Birmingham 35244; 800-987-6277 or 205-987-7132

AK: **Alaska HomeSpun Educators**, PO Box 798, Girdwood 99587

Homeschoolers Unlimited, 392D Kenal Av, Ft Richardson 99505-1227; 907-428-1022

Sitka Home Educators, PO Box 1191, Sitka 99835

AZ: Arizona Families for Home Education, PO Box 2035, Chandler 85244-2035; 800-929-3927

Bethany Home Educators, 2720 S Flint Cir, Mesa 85202

East Valley Educators (Phoenix/Metro area), Sue 480-983-5660 or Sylvia 480-987-1404

Phoenix Learning Alternatives Network, 8835 N 47th Pl, Phoenix 85028; 602-483-3381

SPICE, 10414 W Mulberry Dr, Avondale 85323

Telao Home Educators 520-749-4757 (Tucson)

AR: Coalition of AR Parents, PO Box 192455, Little Rock 72219; 501-888-1942

CA: California Homeschool Network, PO Box 55485, Hayward 94545-0485; 1-800-327-5339

Esparto Homeschoolers, PO Box 305, Esparto 95627; 530-787-3613

Home School Association of CA (formerly Northern CA Homeschool Association), PO Box 2442, Atascadero 93423-2442; 888-HSC-4440; web page www.hsc.org

Homeschooling Coop of Sacramento, 15 Moses Ct, Sacramento 95823-6368

Humboldt Homeschoolers, PO Box 2125, Trinidad 95570; 707-677-3290

Los Angeles Homeschoolers, PO Box 1166, Malibu 90265; 310-456-3845

Mountain View Park Homeschoolers, 6603 Mammoth Av, Van Nuys 91405-4813

North Santa Clara Valley Homeschoolers, 795 Sheraton Dr, Sunnyvale 94087

Peninsula Homeschoolers, 4795 Lage Dr, San Jose 95130; 408-379-6835

Riverside Area Home Learners, 731 Mt Whitney Cir, Corona 91719; 909-279-4026

San Diego Home Educators, 619-281-6581

San Francisco Homeschoolers, c/o Anne Donjacour, 41 Eastwood Dr, San Francisco 94112-1225

School of Home Learning Support Group, 1904 Flora Vista St, Needles 92363; 619-326-2107

Sonoma County Homeschoolers Association, 5584 Carriage Ln, Santa Rosa 95403; 707-765-2181

South St Centre, Box 261, Boulder Creek 95006 (resource center for families)

South Valley Homeschoolers Association, Box 961, San Martin 95046

SPICE, c/o PO Box 282, Wilton 95693

Tri-City Homeschoolers, 39195 Levi St, Newark 94560

Wildflower Homeschoolers, 1557 Vancouver Way, Livermore 94550; 925-455-0465

Yosemite Area Homeschoolers, PO Box 74, Midpines 95345

   CO: **Boulder County Home Educators,** c/o Berg, 1495 Riverside, Boulder 80304; 303-449-5916

CO Home Educators' Association, 3043 S Laredo Cir, Aurora

80013; 303-441-9938

CO Home Schooling Network, 7490 W Apache, Sedalia 80135; 303-688-4136

Fall River Homeschool, PO Box 3322, Idaho Springs 80452

Home Educators for Excellence of Durango, c/o Gring, 315 Timberline Dr, Durango 81301

West River Unschoolers, 2420 N 1 St, Grand Junction 81501; 970-241-4137

CT: **Connecticut Home Educators Association**, PO Box 250, Cobalt 06414; 203-781-8569

Unschoolers' Support, 22 Wildrose Av, Guilford 06437; 203-458-7402

DE: **Tri State Homeschoolers Association**, PO Box 7193, Newark 19714-7193

FL: **Florida Parent-Educators Association,** PO Box 1193, Venice 34284-1193; 877-275-3732

Homeschool Network, 548 N Lake Pleasant Rd, Apopka 32712-3904; 407-889-4632

Tallahassee Homeschool Group, 5227 Wild Olive Way, Tallahassee 32310; 850-575-7091

GA: **Atlanta Alternative Education Network**, c/o Sheffield, 1672 Cody Cir, Tucker 30084; 404-636-6348

Cobb County Homeschoolers, 813 Wyntuck Dr, Kennesaw 30144

Harvest Home Educators, PO Box 1756, Buford 30518; 770-455-0449

Home Education Information Resource Center, PO Box 2111, Rosewell 30077-2111; 404-681-HEIR; www.heir.org

North Side Atlanta Homeschoolers, c/o Jane Kelly, 4141 Wieuca, Atlanta 30342

Southern Unschoolers Network, c/o Lorri Jordan, 4617 Stewart Reilly Dr, Acworth 30101; 770-529-1391

Spectrum Homeschoolers, c/o Leslie Montemayor, 3426 Williams Pl, Conyers 30013; 770-760-0518

HI: Christian Homeschoolers of Hawaii, 910824 Oama St, Ewa Beach 96706; 808-689-6398.

Hawaii Homeschool Association, PO Box 3476, Mililani 96789

Hawaii Island Home Educators, 808-968-8076 or 808-965-9002

The Tropical Homeschooler (newsletter), c/o Pinsky, 220 Waipalani Rd, Haiku, Maui 96708; 808-572-9289

IA: IDEA (Iowans Dedicated to Educational Alternatives), c/o Katy Diltz, 3296 Linn-Buchanan Rd, Coggon 52218; 319-224-3675

Iowa Families for Christian Education, RR 3 Box 143, Missouri Valley 51555

ID: Family Unschooling Network, 1809 N 7 St, Boise 83702; 208-345-2703

Home Educators of ID, 3618 Pine Hill Dr, Coeur d'Alene 83814; 208-667-2778

IL: Evanston Home Educators, Maureen O'Grady, 847-676-2440

Homeschooling Families of IL, 630-548-4349 (Naperville)

HOUSE, 9508 Springfield Av Evanston 60203; 847-675-3632 (statewide)

Spectrum Homeschoolers, c/o Karolyn Kuehner, 10859 S. Longwood Dr, Chicago 60643-3312; 773-779-7608

IN: Families Learning Together, c/o Jill Whelan, 1714 E 51 St, Indianapolis 46205; 317-255-9298

IN Association of Home Educators, 850 N Madison Av, Greenwood 46142; 317-859-1202

Michiana LIFE (Learning in Family Environment), c/o Nancy Sawyer, 2736 Southridge Dr, South Bend 46614; www.onelist.com/subscribe/Michiana-LIFE (includes families in SW Michigan)

Wabash Valley Homeschool Association, c/o Palmer, 2515 E Quinn Av, Terre Haute 47805; 812-466-9467

KS: Central KS Homeschoolers, c/o Susan Peach, Rt 1 Box 28A, Rush Center 67575

Christian Home Educators Confederation of KS, PO Box 3564, Shawnee Mission 66203; 316-945-0810

Lawrence Area Unaffiliated Group of Homeschoolers, c/o Michener, RR 1 Box 496, Perry 66073

Teaching Parents Association, PO Box 3968, Wichita 67201; 316-945-0810

KY: KY Home Education Association, PO Box 81, Winchester 40392-0081

Madison County Homeschool Association, 239 Reeves Rd, Richmond 40475

LA: Southwest Acadiana Homeschoolers, 507 S. Arenas, Rayne 70578; 318-334-2812

Wild Azalea Unschoolers, 6055 General Meyer Av, New Orleans 70131; 504-392-5647

ME: **ME Homeschool Association**, PO Box 421, Topsham 04086; 800-520-0577

Peninsula Area Homeschooling Association, PO Box 235, Deer Isle 04627

Sebago Lake Homeschoolers Support Group, RR 2 Box 54, Sebago Lake 04075; 207-642-4368

Southern ME Home Education Support Network, 76 Beech Ridge Rd, Scarborough 04074; 207-883-9621

Western Washington Cty Homeschoolers, RFD 1 Box 93, Harrington 04643

MD: **Educating Our Own**, 686 Geneva Dr, Westminster 21157; 410-857- 0168

Family Unschoolers Network News, 1688 Belhaven Woods Ct, Pasadena 21122-3727

Glen Burnie Home School Support Group, c/o Whetzel, 6514 Dolphin Ct, Glen Burnie 21061

Maryland Home Education Association, 9085 Flamepool Way, Columbia 21045; 410-730-0073

Maryland-Pennsylvania Home Educators, see under Pennsylvania

North County Home Educators and **Family Unschoolers Network,** 1688 Belhaven Woods Ct, Pasadena 21122-3727

Prince George's Home Learning Network, 3730 Marlborough Way, College Park 20740; Jacqui Walpole 301-935-5456; Sydney Jacobs 301-431-1838

MA: **ALOHA** (A Loosely Organized Homeschool Association), c/o Hazelton, 24A Calamint Rd N, Princeton 01541; 978-464-7794

Alternative Ways of Learning (unschooling group), PO Box 1274, Charlton City 01508; 508-248-7182

Apple Country Homeschooling Association, PO Box 246, Harvard 01451; 978-456-8515

Berkshire Homeschoolers Group, 217 Old State Rd, Berkshire 01224; 413-443-1770

Cape Ann Homeschoolers, 108R Main St, Rockport 01966; 978-546-7125

Franklin County Homelearning Families, Jean Johnson, 72 Prospect St, Greenfield 01301; 413-773-9280

Greater Boston Home Educators, 781-246-2059 (Wakefield)

Groton-Dunstable Home Educators, c/o Leslie McLeod-Warrick, 663 Townsend Rd, Groton 01450; 978-448-0929

Homeschoolers of MA Education Club (Boston area), contact Phoebe Wells, 617-876-7273

Homeschooling Together (Arlington/Belmont area), Sophia Sayigh 781-641-0566

Lowell area group, Debbie Finch, 978-458-3896

Mass. Home Educators, 22 Garland St, Lynn 01902; 781-599-6267

Mass. Home Learning Assoc, PO Box 1558 Marstons Mills 02648; eastern Mass. contact Loretta Heuer 508-429-1436; western Mass. Kathy Smith 978-249-9056; www.mhla.org

Medway/Mills Support Group, 508-359-5910

Newburyport Area Homeschool Network, 32 Columbus Av, Newburyport 01950; 978-462-5680

North Shore Support Group, 978-468-4663 or 978-658-8970

Pathfinder Learning Center, PO Box 804, Amherst 01002; 413-253-9412

Plymouth PALS, Eileen Fortunato 508-747-0297

SE Massachusetts Homeschool Assoc, PO Box 4336, Fall River 02723-0403; 508-672-0248

Wakefield area group, Lucia Jenkins 781-246-2059

MI: **Benzie Home Educators**, PO Box 208, Benzonia 49616

Families Learning and Schooling at Home (FLASH), 21671 B Drive N, Marshall 45068; 616-781-1069

Heritage Home Educators, 2122 Houser Rd, Holly 48442

Home Educators' Circle, 1280 S John Hix, Westland 48186; 313-326-5406

Info Network for Christian Homes, 4150 Ambrose NE, Grand Rapids 49505

Older Homeschoolers Group, c/o Linn Family, 9120 Dwight Dr, Detroit 48214; 313-331-8406

OWL (Oakland, Washtenaw, Livingston) Homeschool Support Group, c/o Debra Cohn, 6036 Seven Mile, S Lyon 48178; 810-437-8931

Sault Home Education Association, 1102 Ashmun, Sault Ste Marie 49783

Sunnyridge Alternative Learning Center, HCO 1 Box 134, Pelkie 49958

MN: **Fargo-Moorehead Homeschool Association**, 1909-8th St S, Moorehead 56560

MN Homeschoolers Alliance, PO Box 23072; Richfield 55423; 612-288-9662

MS: **Home Educators of Central Mississippi,** 4083 Robin Dr, Jackson 39206; 601-366-9218

Oxford Homeschool Network, 21 CR 3024, Oxford 38655

MO: LEARN, PO Box 10105, Kansas City 64171; 913-383-7888; www.kclearn.org (includes families in KS)

Ozark Lore Society, c/o Eisenmann, HC 73 Box 160, Drury 65638; 417-679-3391 (Ozark area group)

SHELL (Springfield Home Education: Learning for a Lifetime), c/o Donna Culbertson, PO Box 1412, Springfield 65801; 417-767-2214

St. Louis Homeschool Network, Karen Karabell, 4147 W Pine, St. Louis 63108; 314-534-1171

MT: **Bozeman Homeschool Network,** c/o Lora Dalton, 201 S 6 Av Apt A, Bozeman 59715; 406-586-3499

Mid-Mountain Home Education Network, PO Box 2182, Montana City Station, Clancy 59634; 406-443-3376

Montana Coalition of Home Educators, PO Box 43, Gallatin Gateway 59730; 406-587-6163

NE: LEARN, 7741 E Avon Ln, Lincoln 68505; 402-488-7741

NV: **Home Schools United/Vegas Valley,** PO Box 93564, Las Vegas 89193-3564; 702-870-9566

NH: **New Hampshire Home School Coalition,** PO Box 2224, Concord 03302; 603-539-7233

NJ: **Central Jersey Homeschoolers,** 23D Franklin St, South Bound Brook 08880

Educational Excellence-School at Home, PO Box 771, Summit 07901

Families Learning Together, PO Box 8041, Piscataway 08855-8001; 732-968-5143

Homeschoolers of Central NJ, 116 Mountain View Rd, Princeton 08540; 609-333-1119

North Jersey Home Schoolers Association, 44 Oak St, Hillsdale 07642; 201-666-6025

The Tutor, 1239 Whitaker Av, Millville 08332; 609-327-1224

Unschoolers Network, 2 Smith St, Farmingdale 07727; 908-938-2473 (statewide)

NM: **Glorieta Family Educators**, Star Rt 1 Box 404, Glorieta 87535

Home Educators of Santa Fe, 21 Frasco Rd, Santa Fe 87505; 505-466-4462

Homeschooling PACT, c/o Senn, Box 961, Portales 88130; 505-359-1618

Unschoolers of Albuquerque, 2905 Tahiti CT NE, Albuquerque 87112; 505-299-2476

NY: **APPLE** (Attachment & Positive Parenting & Lovingly Educating) **Family and Homeschool Group**, PO Box 2036, N Babylon 11703; 516-243-1944

Families for Home Education, 3219 Coulter Rd, Cazenovia 13035; 315-655-2574

Fingerlakes Unschoolers Network, 5331 Heverly Rd, Trumansburg 14886; 607-387-3001

Greater Southern Tier Homeschoolers, Nichele Neurauter, 1560 Red School Rd, Corning 14830; 607-524-6345

Homeschoolers Network of the Mid-Hudson Valley, RD 2 Box 211P, Ski Run Rd, Bloomingburg NY 12721; 914-733-1002

Lake to Lake Homeschoolers (Geneva), c/o Julie Burgess, 1399 Maryland Rd, Phelps 14532; 315-548-4026

Long Island Homeschoolers Association, 4 Seville Pl, Massapequa Park 11762; 516-795-5554

New York City Home Educators Alliance, PO Box 1214 Murray Hill Station, NY 10156; 212-505-9884

New York Home Educators' Network, Anne Hodge, 39 North St, Saratoga Spgs 12866; 518-584-9110 (statewide)

OASIS (Oneonta area Sharing in Schooling), PO Box 48, Gilbertsville 13776; 607-783-2271

Rochester Area Homeschoolers Association, 275 Yarmouth Rd, Rochester 14610; 716-271-0845

Western NY Homeschoolers, Gloria Zemer, 18 Maple Av, Portville 14770; 716-933-8669

Woodstock Home Educators Network, 12 Cantines Isl, Saugerties 12477; 914-247-0319

NC: **Families Learning Together**, 1670 NC 33 West, Chocowinity 27817

North Carolinians for Home Education, 419 N Boylan Av, Raleigh 27603-1211; 919-834-NCHE

ND: **ND Home School Association**, PO Box 486, Mandan 58554; 701-223-4080

OH: **Christian Parents Association**, 310 Bluebonnet Dr, Findlay 45840 (local only)

Families Unschooling in the Neighborhood (FUN), 3636 Paris Blvd, Westerville 43081; 614-794-2171

Growing Together, c/o Nancy McKibben 1676 Trendril Ct,

Columbus 43229

Heights Homeschoolers, 2065 Halsey, S Euclid 44118

HELP Northwest Ohio, 3905 Herr Rd, Sylvania 43560; 419-843-7179

Home Education League of Parents (Central Ohio), PO Box 14296, Columbus 43214; 614-470-2219

Home Education Resource Center of Central OH, c/o Belinda Augustus, 1713 Keeler Ct, Columbus 43227; 614-237-0004

Home Education Resource Organization, 170 W Main St, Norwalk 44857; 419-663-1064

Home School Network of Greater Cincinnati, 2115 Harcourt Dr, Cincinnati 45244; 513-683-1279 or 513-772-9579

LIFE (Learning in Family Environments) Support Group, PO Box 2512, Columbus 43216; 614-241-6957

OH Home Educators Network, PO Box 23054, Chagrin Falls 44023-0054; 330-274-0542

Parents Enriching Alternative Childhood Education, 9520 Co Rd 10-2, Delta 43515; 337-4810

OK: **Cornerstone** (Tulsa area), PO Box 459, Sperry 74073; 918-425-4162

Home Educators Resource Organization, Rt 1 Box 40C,Cleo Springs 73729; 918-396-0108. Statewide group supporting unschooling

OR: **HomeSource,** PO Box 40884, Eugene OR 97404; 541-689-1051

Greater Portland Homeschoolers, PO Box 82415, Portland 97282; 503-241-5350

The Learning Connection, PO Box 1091 #196, Grants Pass 97526; 541-476-5686

Oregon Home Education Network, 4470 SW Hall Blvd #286, Beaverton 97005; 503-321-5166

PA: **Chester County Homeschoolers**, 226 Liandoverry, Exton 19341

Diversity United in Homeschooling, 233 Bluebell Av. Langhorne 19047; 215-428-3865

Maryland-Pennsylvania Home Educators, PO Box 67, Shrewsbury 17361; 717-993-3603

PA Home Education Network, 285 Allegheny St, Meadville 16335; 412-561-5288

PA Homeschoolers, RD 2 Box 117, Kittanning 16201; 412-783-6512

People Always Learning Something (PALS), 105 Marie Dr, Pittsburgh 15237; 412-367-6240

Valley Unschoolers Network (Lehigh Valley area), c/o Kiernan, 4458 Coffeetown Rd, Schnecksville 18078; 610-799-2742

RI: **Parent Educators of RI**, PO Box 782, Glendale 02826

Rhode Island Guild of Home Teachers (Home Spun News), Box 11, Hope RI 02831; 401-821-7700

SC: **Carolina SuperSchoolers**, 777 Hillview St, Spartanburg 29302

Home Organization of Parent Educators, c/o Griesemer, 1697 Dotterer's Run, Charleston 29414; 763-7833

Teacher's Ink (formerly Homeschool Association of SC), PO Box 13386, Charleston 29422; 803-795-9982

South Carolina Association of Independent Home Schools, PO Box 2104, Irmo 29063

South Carolina Homeschool Alliance, 1679 Memorial Park Rd, Suite 179, Lancaster 29720

SD: **South Dakota Home School Association,** PO Box 882, Sioux Falls 57101; 605-335-1125

TN: **Home Education Association of Tenn** (HEAT), 3677 Richbriar Ct, Nashville 37211

TX: **Austin Area Homeschoolers,** 510 Park Blvd, Austin 78751

Houston Alternative Education Alliance, 12811 Ivy Forest Dr, Cypress 77429

Houston Unschoolers Group, Holly Furgason, 9625 Exeter Rd, Houston 77093; 713-695-4888;

North Texas Self-Educators, c/o Jordan, 150 Forest Ln, Double Oak/Lewisville 75067; 817-430-4835

Texas Homeschool Coalition, PO Box 6982, Lubbock 79493; 806-797-4927

UT: **Salt Lake Home Educators,** 6522 Appomattox Way, Taylorville 84123; 801-269-1997

Utah Home Education Association, PO Box 570218, Sigurd 84657-0218; 801-535-1533

VT: **Ottaquechee Homeschoolers,** 1618 Westerdale Rd, Woodstock 05091; Jessica 802-457-1993

Resource Center for Homeschooling, PO Box 55, Fairfax 05454; 802-849-2906

Windham County Homeschoolers, RR 2 Box 1332, Putney 05346

VA: ALOFT (Alt. Learning Options for Free Thinkers), 2120 Wiggington Rd, Lynchburg 24502

Blue Ridge Area Network for Congenial Homeschooling, c/o Amy Birdwell, 255 Ipswich Pl, Charlottesville 22901

Christ-Centered Home Educators, 3601 Plank Rd, PMB 323, Fredericksburg VA 22407; 540-898-0920

Home Educators Network, 3320 Waverly Dr, Fredericksburg 22401

Home Instruction Support Group, 217 Willow Terr, Sterling 22170

LEARN/No. VA Homeschoolers, c/o Vernon, 1111 Waynewood Blvd, Alexandria 22308

Learning in a Family Environment (LIFE), 40672 Tankerville Rd, Lovettsville 20180

VA Home Education Association, Rt 1 Box 370, Gordonsville 22942; 540-832-3578

WA: Clark County Home Educators, PO Box 5941, Vancouver 98668

Families Learning Together, Box 10 Tiger Star Rt, Colville 99114

Family Academy, 146 SW 153rd #290, Seattle 98166

Family Learning Organization, PO Box 7247, Spokane 99207; 509-467-2552 (also statewide)

Homeschoolers' Support Association, PO Box 413, Maple Valley 98038; 253-891-0384

Palouse Home Learning Alternatives, SE 405 Hill, Pullman 99163

Rainbow Way Playgroup, c/o Bystrom, 8632 Inverness Dr

NE, Seattle 98115-3936; 206-522-4313

Seattle Homeschool Group, 819 NE 84, Seattle 98115; 425-402-9048

Teaching Parents Association, PO Box 1934, Woodinville 98072-1934; 425-739-8562

Washington Homeschool Organization, 6632 S 191 Pl Suite E100, Kent 98032-2117; 425-251-0439

Whatcom Homeschool Association, 3851 Britton Rd, Bellingham 98226

WV: **West VA Home Educators Association**, PO Box 3707, Charleston 25337-3707; 1-800-736-9843

WI: **Families in Schools at Home** (FISH), 4639 Conestoga Trail, Cottage Grove 53527

HOME (Madison Chapter), 5745 Bittersweet Pl, Madison 53705; 608-238-3302

Unschooling Families, 1908 N. Clark St, Appleton 54911; 414-735-9832

Wisconsin Parents Association, PO Box 2502, Madison 53701

WY: **Unschoolers of Wyoming**, 429 Hwy 230, #20, Laramie 82070

NATIONAL HOMESCHOOL GROUPS AND PUBLICATIONS

American Homeschool Association, PO Box 1125, Republic WA 99166-1125; 509-486-2477

Catholic Home School Newsletter, 688 11th Ave NW, New Brighton MN 55112

The Drinking Gourd (homeschoolers of color), PO Box 2557, Redmond WA 98073

Gentle Spirit, PO Box 246, Wauna, WA 98395; 425-747-7703; www.gentlespirit.com

Heart of Homeschooling, ed. Shari Henry, PO Box 1055, Madison AL 35758 (based on ideas of R. Moore, C. Mason)

Holt Associates/Growing Without Schooling, 2380 Massachusetts Ave, Suite 104, Cambridge MA 02140; 617-864-3100; www.holtgws.com

Home Education Magazine, PO Box 1083, Tonasket WA 98855; www.home-ed-magazine.com

Home School Legal Defense Association, PO Box 159, Paeonian Springs VA 22129; 540-338-5600

Homeschool Support Network, PO Box 1056, Gray ME 04039; 207-657-2800

Homeschooling Today, PO Box 1425 Melrose FL 32666

Home Educator's Family Times, PO Box 708, Gray ME 04039; 207-657-2800

Moore Report International, Box 1, Camas, WA 98607

National Center for Home Education, PO Box 200, Paeonian Spgs VA 22129; 540-338-7600

National Home Education Research Institute, Western Baptist College, 5000 Deer Park Dr SE, Salem OR 97301-9392; 503-375-7019. Publishes *Home School Researcher.*

National Homeschool Association, PO Box 327, Webster NY 14580-0327; 513-772-9580

Practical Homeschooling, PO Box 1250 Fenton MO 63026

The Teaching Home, PO Box 20219, Portland OR 97220-0219

SPECIAL-INTEREST HOMESCHOOLING GROUPS

At Our Own Pace, c/o Jean Kulczyk, 102 Willow Dr, Waukegan IL 60087; 847-662-5432 (newsletter for homeschooling families with special needs)

The Drinking Gourd (homeschoolers of color), PO Box 2557, Redmond WA 98073; 206-836-0336 or 1-800-TDG-5487

Home School Association for Christian Science Families, 445 Airport Rd, Tioga TX 76271

Homeschoolers for Peace & Justice, PO Box 74, Midpines CA 95345

Homeschoolers Travel Network, NHA,10755 Hibner Rd, Hartland MI 48353

Homeschooling Unitarian Universalists and Humanists, 3135 Lakeland Dr, Nashville TN 37214-3312; 615-889-4938

Islamic Homeschool Association of North America, 1312 Plymouth Ct, Raleigh NC 27610

Jewish Home Educator's Network, c/o Kander, 2122 Houser, Holly MI 48442

National Association of Catholic Home Educators, 6102 Saints Hill Ln, Broad Run VA 22014; 540-349-4314

National Association of Mormon Home Educators, 2770 S 1000 West, Perry UT 84302

National Challenged Homeschoolers Association (NATH-HAN), 5383 Alpine Rd SE, Olalla WA 98359; 206-857-4257

National Handicapped Homeschoolers Association, 814 Shavertown Rd, Boothwyn PA 19061; 215-459-2035

HOMESCHOOL GROUPS OUTSIDE OF U.S.

Canada

Alberta Home Education Association, c/o Aine Stasiewich, Box 3451, Leduc AB T9E 6M2

Alternative Education Resource Association, 11 Mosely Close, Red Deer AB T4N 5S8

Calgary Home Educators Encouragement & Resource Society, RR 6, Calgary AB T2M 4L5

Canadian Alliance of Homeschoolers, 272 Hwy #5, RR 1, St George, ON NOE 1NO; 519-448-4001

Canadian Home Educators Association of BC, 4684 Darin Ct, Kelowna BC V1W 2B3; 604-764-7462

Community Connections, BJ Smith, 225 37 St NW, Calgary AB T2N 4N6

Cowichan Valley Homelearners Support Group, RR 7, Duncan BC V9L 4W4

Cowichan Valley Christian Homelearners Support Group, 1050 Marchmont Rd, Duncan BC V9L 2M7

Educare: Homeschooling News, Box 23021, Woodstock ON N4T 1R9

Education Advisory, 2267 Kings Ave, W Vancouver BC V7V 2C1

Greater Vancouver Home Learners Support Group, 604-228-1939; 604-298-6710

Home Education News, Box 39009 Pt Grey RPO, Vancouver BC V6R 4P1

Home Learning Resource Centre, Box 61, Quathiaski BC V0P 1N0

Home School Legal Defense Association of Canada, PO Box 42009, Millbourne PO, Edmonton AB T6K 4C4; 403-986-1566

Homebased Learning Society of Alberta, 8754 Connors Rd, Edmonton AB T6C 4B6; 988-4652

Homeschoolers Association of North Alberta, 6311 14 Av, Edmonton AB T6L 1Y1

Manitoba Association for Schooling at Home, 89 Edkar Cres, Winnipeg MB R2G 3H8

Montreal Homeschoolers' Support Group, 5241 Jacques Grenier, Montreal PQ H3W 2G8

Montreal Metropolitan Support Group; www.angelfire.

National Capital Region Home Based Learning Network, 136 Aylmer Av, Ottawa K1S 2Y2; www.flora.org/hbln

New Brunswick Association of Christian Homeschoolers, RR 1 Site 11 Box 1, Hillsborough NB E0A 1X0; 506-734-2863

Nova Scotia Home Education Association, c/o Marion Homer, RR 1, Rose Bay B0J 2X0; 902-766-4355

Nova Scotia Support Group, c/o Laura Uhlman RR 1, Pleasantville NS B0R 1G0

Ontario Federation of Teaching Parents, 83 Fife Rd, Guelph ON N1H 6X9; 519-763-1150

Ontario Homeschoolers, Box 19, Gilford, ON L0L 1R0; 705-456-3186

Orilla Homeschoolers' Support Group, 45 Albert St North, Orilla ON L3V 5K3

Quebec Homeschooling Advisory, CP 1278, 1002 Rosemarie, Val David PQ J0T 2N0

Rideau Valley Home Educators Association, c/o Dubuc, 1144 Byron Av, Ottawa ON K2B 6T4; 613-729-0117

Salt Spring Unschoolers Network, 132 Bullock Creek Rd, Salt Spring Island BC V8K 2L3

Saskatchewan Home-Based Educators, 116A Idylwyld Dr. N, suite 13, Saskatoon SK S7L 0Y7

Tri-City Home Learners Network, 604-464-1056 (Port Coquitlan, BC)

Victoria Home Learning Network, 106-290 Regina, Victoria, BC V8Z 6S6

Villa Villekula Homeschool Resource Group, 1250 Gladstone Av, Windsor ON N8X 3H3; 519-254-3593

Wondertree Education Society, Box 38083, Vancouver BC V5Z 4L9; 604-739-5943

Yukon Home Educators' Society, Box 4993, Whitehorse YT Y1A 4S2

Australia

Accelerated Christian Education, PO Box 10, Strathpine, Queensland 07 205 7503

Alternative Education Resource Group, PO Box 71, Chirnside Park VIC 3116

Brisbane Homeschooling Group, Lot 2, Caboolture River Rd, Upper Caboolture 4510

Canberra Home Education Network, 23 Bardolph St, Bonython, ACT 2905, 9

Homeschoolers Australia Party Limited, PO Box 420, Kellyville 2153, NSW Australia

NSW Central Coast Homeschool Group, RMB 6346, MacDonalds Rd, Lisarow NSW 2250, Australia

Sunshine Coast Homeschooling Group, #40 Browns Rd, Belli Park via Edmundi, 4562 Queensland

Yarra Valley Homeschoolers, 9 Salisbury St, Warburton

England

Education Otherwise, PO Box 7420, London N9 9SG; (tel.) 0891 518303 (has local contacts throughout England and the U.K.)

France

Homeschooling Bulletin, c/o Sophie Haesen, 7 rue de la Montagne, F-68480 Vieux Ferrette

L'Ecole a la Maison, c/o Nadine Stewart, 6 Grande Rue, F-38660 Le Touvet

Les Enfants D'Abord, c/o Shosha, 4 rue de Lergue, F-34800 Brignac

Hong Kong

Discovery Bay Homeschoolers of Hong Kong, General POB 12114, Hong Kong, China

Ireland

Home Education Network, Knockroe, Borris, Co Carlow; tel. (+353)-1-282-9638; www.ie.embnet.org/hen/

Japan

Otherwise Japan, PO Box Kugayama, Suginami-ku, Tokyo, Japan; email owj@tkb.att.ne.jp

Netherlands

Netherlands Homeschoolers, Raadhuislaan 31, 2131 Hoofddoorp, The Netherlands

New Zealand

Home Educator's Network of Aotearoa, PO Box 11-645, Ellerslie 1131, Auckland

Homeschooling Federation of New Zealand, PO Box 41-226, St. Lukes, Auckland

The New Zealand Home Schooling Association, 5 Thanet Av, Mt Albert, Auckland, New Zealand

South Africa

National Coalition of Home Schoolers, PO Box 14, Dundee, 3000. tel. 0341 23712, email durham@liadun.dundee.lia.net

Spain

Crecer Sin Escuela, c/o Szil-Norberg, Apartado 45, Alfaz del Pi 03580, Alicante, Spain

Sweden

MATS, c/o Wilson, Atelji Italienska Palatset, JF Liedholmsvag, 17352 34, Vaxjo, Sweden; tel. 0470 74 97 74; email remus.wilson@vaxjo.mai.telia.com

OTHER ORGANIZATIONS

These educational, child-raising, or self-reliance organizations are good sources of help and allies. Again, a SASE is appreciated.

Alliance for Parental Involvement in Education, PO Box 59, E Chatham NY 12060-0059; 518-392-6900 (deals with public, private, and home schools)

Alternative Education Resource Organization, 417 Roslyn Rd, Roslyn Hghts NY 11577; 516-621-2195

La Leche League International, 1400 N Meacham Rd, PO Box 4079, Schaumberg IL 60168-4079; 1-800-LA LECHE

National Association for the Legal Support of Alt. Schools, PO Box 2823, Santa Fe NM 87501; 505-471-6928

National Center for Fair and Open Testing (FairTest), 342 Broadway, Cambridge MA 02139; 617-864-4810

National Coalition Of Alternative Community Schools, PO Box 15036, Santa Fe NM 87506; 505-474-4312

These lists may be reproduced in full or in part only if the source is credited as *"Growing Without Schooling,* 2380 Massachusetts Avenue, Suite 104, Cambridge MA 02140."

APPENDIX THREE

LEARNING MATERIALS LIST

This is a list of all learning materials and resources that have been mentioned in *Growing Without Schooling* since issue #1 (over the years we have deleted materials that are no longer available). In addition, it includes quite a few items that we have not written about in *GWS* (though we yet may), but which we feel comfortable recommending to you.

This is just a sampling to help jump-start your thinking about what is available for you to use at home with your children. Many of the books and magazines I've listed throughout this book contain different resources.

If an item on this list has been mentioned in GWS, you'll find issue and page number at the end of the listing. For example, "34p6" means "See GWS #34, page 6."

As with all our resource lists, we'd like to keep this current, so please send us changes if you learn of any.

Arts, Crafts, Films

KidsArt News, PO Box 274, Mt Shasta CA 96067; phone/fax 530-926-5076; www.kidsart.com . Series of art teaching booklets. Children's art supplies catalog. www.kidsart.com 49p11.

NASCO Arts & Crafts, 901 Janesville Av, Ft Atkinson WI 53538; 920-563-2446. Free catalog.

Sculpture House, 100 Camp Meeting Ave., Skillman NJ 08558; 609-466-2986. Clay, supplies. 40p20.

Books, Games, Learning Materials

American Audio Prose Library, PO Box 842, Columbia MO 65205; 1-800-447-2275; www.americanaudieprose.com. Authors on tape. 69p27.

American Printing House for the Blind, 1839 Frankfort Av, Louisville KY 40206; 502-895-2405. Cranmer Abacus, books and materials. 57p25.

Animal Town Game Co, PO Box 485, Healdsburg CA 95448; 800-445-8642. Cooperative board games & books. 19p18.

Aristoplay, PO Box 7645, Ann Arbor MI 48107. "Music Maestro" and other educational board games. 131p28.

Ball-Stick-Bird Reading System, Bx 13, Colebrook, CT 06021; 860-738-8871. Phonics using science fiction adventures. 51p24, 54p20, 55p21.

Booklist, American Library Assn, 50 E Huron St, Chicago IL 60611;.312-944-6780 "Purchasing an Encyclopedia: 12 points to consider," $4.95. 54p19.

Bright Baby Books, 101 Star Ln, Whitethorn CA 95589. 707-986-7693. Videos about movement, games to play with infants, and books.

Center for Innovation in Education, 1500–A, Dell. Ave., Campbell, CA 95008-6901; 800-395-6088. Math, reading.

Creative Kids, HC03, Box 9550-S, Palmer, AK 99645; 907-745-3769; Fax: 907-746-3073; School supplies to home-schooling families.

Chinaberry Book Service, 2780 Via Orange Way, Suite B, Spring Valley CA 91978. Catalog of books. 57p26.

Cricket, 1058 8th St, La Salle IL 6130; 800-776-22421. Children's magazine. 7p8.

Cuisenaire Co of America, PO Box 5026, White Plains, NY 10602–5026. Math & science materials & books. 23p22.

Family Pastimes, RR 4, Perth, Ontario K7H 3C6; 613-267-4819. Cooperative board games. 13p2; 131p28.

Follett Educational Service, 1433 Internationale Parkway, Woodridge, IL 60517; 800-621-4272 or 1474. Used texts. Give school name. 40p20.

Freebies Magazine,1135 Eugenia Place. PO Box 310, Carpinteria, VCCA 93014; 805-566-1225. $8.95/5 iss. 51p26.

Frank Schaffer Publications, 23740 Hawthorne Blvd., Torrance, CA 90505. Educational materials for ages 3-14. 800-421-5565; Fax: 800-837-7260; www.frankschaffer.com

Front Row Experience, 540 Discovery Bay Blvd, Byron CA 94514-9454; 800-524-9091. Materials about movement education, perceptual-motor development, coordination activities for pre-school-6th grade age group.

Gamewright, PO Box 370219, W. Hartford CT 06137; 203-586-8173.

A Gentle Wind, Box 3103, Albany NY 12203; 888-386-7664; www.gentlewind.com. Stories and songs on cassette. 57p26.

Gifted Education Press, 10201 Yuma Court, Manassas VA 20109; 703-369-5017; www.giftededpress.com. Free newsletter.

Guide to Learning, South Carolina Educational TV, PO Box 11000, 1101 George Rogers Blvd., Columbia SC; 1-800-277-0829. Free booklet. 91p27.

Burt Harrison & Co, Inc., PO Box 732, Weston MA 02493-0732. Science manipulatives. 15p9.

Hearthsong, PO Box 1773, Peoria, IL 61656; 1-800-533-4397. Fax 309-689-3857. Toy/craft catalog for families.

The Horn Book, Inc., 11 Beacon St., Boston MA 02108; 800-325-1170; www.hbook.com. Magazine for children's book recommendations.

I Can Read Books, HarperCollins Children's Books, 1350 Avenue of the Americas, NY NY 10019; 800-242-7737. 39p20.

John Holt's Book Store, 2380 Massachusetts Ave, Suite 104, Cambridge MA 02140. 617-864-3100 (headquarters); Orders only: 888-925-9298. *Growing Without Schooling* magazine; free catalog of innovative books and learning materials.

Johnny's Selected Seeds, Foss Hill Rd, Albion ME 04910; 207-437-4301. Child-sized tools. 75p15.

Key Curriculum Press, PO Box 2304, Berkeley CA 94702. 800-338-7638. Fax: 510-548-0755; web page: www.keypress.com. Miquon math workbooks, math books & software. 14p7, 19p16, 52p24.

Lauri Early Learning Puzzles, PO Box F (Avon Valley Rd), Phillips-Avon ME 04966; 207- 639-2000. Rubber puzzles & educational toys.

Materials for Math Maniacs, Institute for Math Mania, PO Box 910, Montpelier VT 05601. 802-223-5871. Catalog of math materials. 88p27.

Math Products Plus, PO Box 64, San Carlos CA 94070;

650-593-2839. Fax: 650-595-0802. Math books, t-shirts, calendars, novelties.

Mayfair Games, 5211 W. 65th St, Bedford Park, IL 60638. Board games for advanced players. 131p28.

McGuffey's Readers, Mott Media, 112 East Ellen, Fenton MI 48430; 248-685-8773.

Michael Olaf Co, Montessori Store, 65 EricsonCt., Suite 1, Arcata CA 95521; 707-826-1557. Tools, playthings, math manipulatives. Catalog $5. 92p29.

Miquon Math—see Key Curriculum Press.

Montessori Services, 80036 Cleveland Ave., Santa Rosa CA 95401; 707-579-3003. Free supply catalog.

National Storytelling Network (formerly known as National Association for Preservation & Perpetuation of Storytelling) 116 1/2 West Main St., Jonesborough TN 37659; 800-525-4515. Books, tapes. 54p12.

Recorded Books, Inc., 270 Skipjack Rd, Prince Frederick MD 20678; 1-800-638-1304. Novels, classics, history, science, on tape. 105p36.

Resource Games, PO Box 151, Redmond WA 98052; 425-883-3143. Geography game without quizzes. 131p28.

Saxon Math, Saxon Publishers, 2450 John Saxon Blvd., Norman OK 73071; 1-800-264-7019.

Scholastic Book Clubs, PO Box 7503, Jefferson City MO 65102; 573-636-5271. Inexpensive paperbacks. 55p24.

Story Stone, Another Place, Rt 123, Greenville NH 03048. Tapes of stories. 57p26.

Superlearning, 450 7th Av, Ste 500, NY NY 10123; 212-

279-8450. Accelerated learning tapes & books.

Tessellations, 800-665-5341. Geographic puzzles using pattern blocks, tangrams and harder tesselating puzzles. 131p28.

Trumpet Book Club, PO Box 6003, Columbia MO 65205-9888; 800-826-0110. 62p6.

COMPUTERS AND ELECTRONICS

EPIE Institute, 103-3 W Montauk Hwy, Hampton Bays NY 11946. 516-728-9100. Sells CD Rom—Educational software selector with nineteen thousand listings.

EDUCATION

Center for the Study of Reading, U of IL, 51 Gerty Dr, Champaign IL 61820. "Becoming a Nation of Readers," $4.50, other info. 45p1.

Calif High school Proficiency Exam, Dept. of Ed, 721 Capitol Mall, Sacramento CA 95814; 916-657-2277. For early graduation.

ERIC (Educational Resources Information Center) A national information system designed to provide users with ready access to an extensive body of education-related literature. 800-538-3742; www.accesseric.org. 32p8, 79p5.

FAIRTEST, 342 Broadway, Cambridge MA 02139; 781-864-4810; Fax 781-497-2224; www.fairtest.org. Newsletter, reports critical of standardized testing. 57p19; 67p23; 132p19.

Family Policy Compliance Office, US Dept. of Ed, 400 Maryland Ave SW, Washington DC 20202-4605. Access to school records. 202-260-3887; Fax: 202-260-9001; Web page: www.ed.gov.

Montessori World Educational Institute, 3025 Monterey Rd, Atascadero CA 93422; 805-466-2872. http://webs.tcsn.net/mwei. Workshops & Home-Study Courses. 52p19.

Plan-It, Richard Glaubman, Night Owl Press, 819 Cass St, Pt Townsend WA 98368; 360-379-0261. Record-keeping system for homeschoolers. 103p16.

The Teaching Company, 7405 Alban Station Ct., Springfield, VA 22150; 800-TEACH12. High school and college lectures on videotape.

Worldbook-Childcraft International, 4788 Highway 3775, Ft. Worth, TX 76116; 800-794-4737. "Typical Course of Study, K-12," Pamphlet. 20p5.

"What Works," Consumer Info, Pueblo CO 81009. Free. Research on education. 50p1.

Foreign Languages

Bolchazy-Carducci Publishers, 1000 Brown St., Uniti 101, Wauconda IL 60084. Audio cassettes and texts for learning Latin.

Calliope, Rte 3, Box 3395, Saylorsburg, PA 18353. 610-381-2587. Foreign languages materials and imported books for infants to adults.

Editions Champlain, 468 Queen St East, Toronto Ont M5A 1T7. 416-364-4345; Fax: 416-364-8843. French books. 30p16.

French for Tots, OptimaLearning Language Land, Barzak Educational Inst., 885 Olive Ave., Suite A, Novato CA 94945; www.optimalearning.com. 800-672-1717. 74p28.

Imported Books, 2025 W. Clarendon Dr., Dallas TX 75208; 214-941-6497. Children's books, many languages.

La Cité, 2306 Westwood Blvd, Los Angeles CA 90064; 310-475-0658. Source of foreign books. 99p18.

The Learnables, International Linguistics, 3505 E Red Bridge, Kansas City MO 64137. 816-765-8855. Foreign language tapes. 31pl6; 66p9.

Lectorum Publications, 137 W. 14th St., New York, NY 10011; 800-345-5946. Catalog of Spanish children's books and magazines. 74p28.

Mangajin, 1025 Moreland Ave SE, Atlanta GA 30316; 404-622-8995; Fax: 404-622-5322; www.mangajin.com. Magazine of cartoons in Japanese and English. 88p28.

National Library of Canada, Children's Literature Service, 395 Wellington St, Ottawa Ont K1A 0N4. Attn: Irene E. Aubrey. Notable Canadian children's books. 30pl6

Schoenhofs, 76A Mt Auburn St, Cambridge MA 02138. 617-547-8855; www.schoenhofs.com. Source of foreign books. 99p18.

Sky Oaks Productions, PO Box 1102, Los Gatos CA 95031; 408-395-7600. Total Physical Response approach to teaching and learning. 33pl6.

MUSIC

Canyon Records & Indian Arts, 4143 N 16th St, Phoenix AZ 85016; 602-266-4823. Native American music, books.

Homespun Music Tapes, Box 340, Woodstock NY 12498; 914-679-7832; www.homespuntapes.com. Fax: 914-246-5282. Audio and video taped lessons for folk instruments. 40p22.

Lark in the Morning, Box 1176, Mendocino CA 95460; 707-964-5569. Folk music & instruments

Library of Congress, Motion Picture, Broadcasting, and Recorded Sound Division, Washington DC 20540; 202-707–5000. Folk music & literature.

Suzuki Association of the Americas, PO Box 17310, Boulder CO 80308; 3888-378-9854; www.suzukiassociation.org. Suzuki music method Parent/Teacher info packet $2. 24p12.

OPPORTUNITIES AND ACTIVITIES

AFS InterNational Exchange Prog, 310 SW 4th Ave. Ste 630, Portland OR 97204-2608; 800-AFS-INFO. Fax: 503-241-1653p; www.afs.org. Damon Knight, Mgr. Host exchange student, or become one. 52p23.

Appalachian Mountain Club, 5 Joy St, Boston MA 02108. 781-523-0636. Fax: 617-523-0722. Web page: www.outdoors.org. Free junior. naturalist program, educational events for families. 30p12.

Center for Interim Programs, PO Box 2347, Cambridge MA 02238; 781-547-0980. Fax: 781-661-

2864; www.thecia.net/usesinterim. Matchmaker for apprenticeships. 52p10, 72p20.

Chesapeake Bay Foundation, Prince George St., Annapolis MD 21401; 800-445-5572. 126p22.

Country School, Rt 3, Millersburg OH 44654. Farm weeks for children.

Crow Canyon Archaeological Ctr, 23390 County Rd K, Cortez CO 81321; 800-422-8975; www.crowcanyon.org.

Experiment in International Living, Box 676, Kipling Rd, Brattleboro VT 05302-0676; 802-257-7751. 800-345-2929. Cultural immersion home study programs for 3,4,5 weeks in summer to 18 countries. Web page: www.worldlearning.org.

Farm Sanctuary, PO Box 150, Watkins Glen NY 14891. 607-583-2225. Fax: 607-583-2041; www.farmsanctuary.org. H. McNulty, Admin.Dir. Apprenticeships in caring for sick animals. 91p27.

Great Smoky Mountains Institute at Tremont, 9275 Tremont Rd, Townsend TN 37882; 423-448-6709. Naturalist Workshops, programs for teenagers.

Hulbert Outdoor Ctr, RR 1 Box 91A, Fairlee VT 05045. Camp weeks for homeschoolers. 75p26.

Kids for Saving Earth Clubs, PO Box 42111, Plymouth MN 55442; 612-559-0602; www.kidsforsavingearth.org. 95p20.

Maine Organic Farms & Gardeners Association Farm Apprenticeships, Box 2176, Augusta ME 04338; 207-622-3118. 68p27.

Mentor-Apprentice Exchange, Box 405, Canning NS B0P 1H0 Canada. 100p9.

NACUL Environmental Design Center, 592 Main St, Amherst MA 01002; 413-256-8025. Architectural internships. 68p27.

National Association for Cottage Industries, PO Box 14850, Chicago IL 60614; 773-472-8116. 46p6. SASE for info, $3 for newsletter.

National Directory of Internships, National Society for Experiential Education, 3509 Haworth Dr, St 207, Raleigh NC 27609-7229. 100p9.

National Wildlife Federation Wildlife Camp, 1400 16th St NW, Washington DC 20036-2266. Nature Study ages 9-17.

Rightful Passage Adventure Courses, Rainbow's End Rd, Nevada City CA 95959; 530-265-5490; www.oro.net/pathfinder/pf.htm. For homeschooled teens. 114p24.

SERVAS, 11 John St, Rm 407, New York NY 10038; 212-267-0252. Visit or host foreign family. 18p1.

Shelter Institute, 873 US RT 1, Woolwich, ME 04579; 207-267-7938. ME 04530. Classes on home construction, boatbuilding. Free booklist. 35p24. For more home-building schools, see 9p7, 21p6.

Time Out, 619 E Blithedale Av, Suite C, Mill Valley CA 94941; 415-383-1834. Individual consultations re: unusual educational placements, apprenticeships, and internships. 75p26.

Tree People, 12601 Mulholland Dr, Beverly HIlls CA 90210; 818-753-4600.Environmental leadership program. 7p12, 36p14.

U.S. Space Camp, Space & Rocket Ctr, Huntsville AL 35807. 4th grade & up.

PARENTING

Compleat Mother, PO Box 209, Minot ND 58702; 701-852-2822; www.compleatmother.com.

Liedloff Continuum Network, PO Box 1634, Sausalito CA 94966. For people interested in the book *The Continuum Concept.* Newsletter $14/yr. 70p23, 103p33.

Mothering Magazine, PO Box 1690, Santa Fe NM 87504; 505-984-6299. For back issues: 888-984-8116.

Mothers at Home, 8310-A Old Courthouse Rd, Vienna VA 22182; 703-827-5903; www.mah.org. *Welcome Home* newsletter supports mothers who choose to stay at home.

Parents' Choice, 410-532-0727; www.parents-choice.com. Review of children's media. $18/yr.

Shining Star Press, PO Box 206, Goleta CA 93116. Publishers of "The Aware Baby," "Helping Young Children Flourish." 42p31.

SCIENCE AND NATURE

Abrams Planetarium, Mich. State U, E Lansing MI 48824; 517-355-4672. Sky Calendar. 28p12.

American Science & Surplus, 3605 Howard, Skokie IL 60076; www.sciplus.com. Catalog of industrial & scientific materials, reduced from normal list prices. $1. 37p23.

Anatomical Chart Co, 8221 Kimball Av, Skokie IL 60076; 800-621-7500. 69p27.

Around Alone Student Ocean Challenge, PO Box 631, Jamestown, RI 02835; 401-423-3535; www.bwsailing.com/soc.html. 97p34.

Astronomical Society of the Pacific, 390 Ashton Ave, San Francisco CA 94112; 415-337-1100. Free catalog of slides, videos, books, posters, software, sky observing aids.

Carolina Biological Supply Company, 2700 York Rd, Burlington NC 27215; 336-584-0381. Catalog for science teachers. 37p23.

Celestial Products, 20659 St. Louis Rd, Philomont VA 20131; 800-235-3783; www.celestialproducts.com. Sky charts, posters, maps, and books.

Edmund Scientific Co, 101 E Gloucester Pike, Barrington NJ 08007; 609-547-3488. Catalog, $1. 12p10.

Exploratorium Store, 3601 Lyon St, San Francisco CA 94123; 415-561-0372. Hands-on science.

Hawkhill Associates, 125 E Gilman St, Madison WI 53703; 608-251-3934. Science videos.

Marine Science Consortium, Box 16, Enterprise St., Wallops Island VA 23337; 804-824-5636. 126p22.

NASA CORE, Lorain County JVS, 15181 Rt 58 S, Oberlin OH 44074; 440-986-6601. Catalog of materials about space. 65p37.

Ranger Rick's Nature Magazine, National Wildlife Federation, 8925 Leesburg Pike, Vienna VA 22184. 16p14.

Sanctuary Magazine, Massachusetts Audubon Society, South Great Rd, Lincoln MA 01773; 781-259- 9500. April '90 issue on kids working to help the environment. $1 + 65¢ pstg. 75p12.

Skeptical Inquirer, Box 703, Amherst NY 14226; 800-634-1610; www.csicop.org. Looks at claims about paranormal phenomena. $25/yr. 82p29.

3-2-1 Contact, Box 2933, Boulder CO 80321; 363-604-1465. Science magazine of the Children's TV Workshop. 20p17.

TOPS Learning Systems, 10970 S Mulino Rd, Canby OR 97013; 503-263-2040. Science lessons.

"Under the Microscope" videos, J.L. Hudson Seedsman, Star Rt 2 Box 337, La Honda CA 94020. Send $1 for catalog of videos that show bugs, bacteria, crystals, much more, under a microscope. 110p28.

Ursa Major, PO Box 3368, Ashland OR 97520; 1-800-999-3433. Large stencils of world maps and of the night sky. 105p36.

Young Astronauts Council, PO Box 65432, Washington DC 20036. Hands-on activities. 57p28.

Your Big Backyard, National Wildlife Federation, 8925 Leesburg Pike, Vienna VA 22184. Mag. for 3-5 yr olds.

ZooBooks, Wildlife Education Ltd, 12233 Thatcher Ct, Poway, CA 92064; 619-574-7866. 37p23.

SOCIAL STUDIES

Amazon Vinegar & Pickling Works Dry Goods, 2218 East 11th Street Davenport IA 52803; 800-798-7979. Catalog of historical items and books. 81p25.

Black Images Book Company, PO Box 41059, Dallas, TX 75241

Asia for Kids, 4480 Lake Forest Drive, Suite 302,

Cincinnati OH 45242; 513-563-3100. Books, cassettes, software related to Asian cultures. 110p28

Calliope, 30 Grove St, Peterborough NH 03458; 603-924-7209. Children's magazine on Greeks, Romans.

Cobblestone, 30 Grove St, Peterborough NH 03458; 800-821-0115. U.S. history magazine for children. 20pl7.

Faces, 30 Grove St, Peterborough NH 03458. World cultures, anthropology magazine for children.

Hubbard Scientific, PO Box 760, Chippewa Falls WI 54729; 715-723-4427 Raised relief maps, models to use in learning about human body, zoology. 10pll.

League of Women Voters, 1730 M St NW, Suite 1000, Washington DC 20036; 202-429-1965; www.lwv.org. Pamphlets: government, current events.

National Geographic Society, 1145 17th St NW, Washington DC 20036; 202-857-7000. Magazines, including World for children, books, maps. 12pl0.

National Geography Bee, Same as National Geographic Society above. 69p4.

National Women's History Project, 7738 Bell Rd, Winsor CA 95492-8515; 707-838-6000; www.nwhp.org. Materials about women in history; multi-cultural.

Replogle Globes, Inc., 2801 S 25th Av, Broadview IL 60153; 708-343-0900. 69p27.

Resource Center of The Americas 3019 Minnehaha Ave. So., Minneapolis MN 55406; 612-276-0801; www.americas.org/rcta/. K-12 curriculum about the Americas.

Smithsonian Magazine, Arts & Industries Bldg, 900 Jefferson Dr SW, Washington DC 20560; 202-786-2900. 14pl0.

US Government Printing Office Superintendent of Documents, 1510 H St. NW, Washington DC 20005; 202-653-5075. Huge assortment of government publications. 69p27.

Wide World Books & Maps, 4411 A Wallingford Ave., Seattle WA 98103; 206-634-3453 ext. 18.

Young Entrepreneur, KidsWay Foundation, 5587 Peachtree Rd, Chamblee GA 30341; 1-888-KidsWay; www.kidsway.com. News magazine, curriculum, books. 117p27.

Special Needs

Deaf Homeschool Resouce, c/o Marilyn Agenbroad, 116 Jerome, Silverton OR 97381; 503-873-8451. 129p14

Deaf Moms Homeschooling Newsletter, c/o Vanessa Kramer, 602 S. West St., Carlinsville IL 62626. 129p14

Hadley School for the Blind, PO Box 299, Winnetka IL 60093; 847-446-6175. Free correspondence courses for visually-impaired children and their parents. 72p7.

National Association for the Deaf, 814 Thayer Av, Silver Spg MD 20910; 301-587-1788. Sign language videos, books. 52p24.

Twins Magazine, 5350 South Roslyn St #400, Englewood CO 80111; 888-558-9467.

WRITING

Child's Play Touring Theatre, 2518 West Armitage, Chicago IL 60647; 773-235-8911; 800-353-3402; www.cptt@sprynet.com. Develops plays out of stories and poems by kids. 77p13.

Educators Publishing Service, 31 Smith Place, Cambridge MA 02138. 617-547-6706. Keyboarding Exchange (typing book), educational books, workbooks, and materials.

Expository Writing Tutorial-by-Mail, Johns Hopkins U, 3400 N Charles St, Baltimore MD 21218; 410-516-8427.

Heinemann Educational Books, 361 Hanover St, Portsmouth NH 03801; 800-541-2086. Videos, books on writing. 54p11.

The Letter Exchange, PO Box 2930, Santa Rosa CA 95605; 707-463-3651. Pen pals, by interests. All ages.

Market Guide for Young Writers, by Kathy Henderson (check your local library or bookstore)

Skipping Stones, PO Box 3939, Eugene OR 97403; 541-342-4956. Multi-ethnic magazine of children's writing.

Stone Soup, PO Box 83, Santa Cruz CA 95063; 800-447-4569. Children's literary magazine.

Teachers & Writers Collaborative, 5 Union Sq W, New York NY 10003; 212-691-6590. Catalog of books about writing.

INDEX

An "A" In Life: Famous Homeschoolers, 61
And The Skylark Sings With Me, 38
And What About College?, 16, 60, 62
The Art of Education, 55
Awakening Your Child's Natural Genius, 55

Bears Guide to Earning College Degrees Nontraditionally, 61
The Big Book of Home Learning, 16, 17
Budgetext Used Textbook Catalog, 55

Child's Work, 37, 47
The Christian Home Educator's Curriculum Manual, 16, 17
Correspondence school, 26, 31, 75
Countdown to Consistency, 55
Curriculum, 2, 8, 17, 30-40, 52, 57, 61, 75, 77, 110-111, 121-122

Deschooling Our Lives, 16
Diplomas, 2, 59

Educating Children at Home, 26

Family Matters: Why Homeschooling Makes Sense, 15
Ferguson's Career Resources Catalog, 61
Freedom Challenge: African American Homeschoolers, 16

Gentle Spirit, 51, 97
Growing Without Schooling/GWS, 3-4, 5, 8, 10, 14, 15, 23, 39, 59, 52, 63, 74, 97, 105, 107, 110

Hard Times In Paradise, 38, 60
The Home Education of a Boy, 71-73
Home Education Magazine, 5, 15, 97
Home Schooling: Parents as Educators, 10
The Homeschool Manual, 15
Homeschooling: See also Learning, Teaching
    Academic Achievement, 10, 24
    College admissions, 59-62
    Course of study, 31, 38, 53-55, 113
    Evaluations, 56-59
    Famous homeschoolers, 60
    Grown Homeschoolers, 59
    High school, 2, 11, 21, 60, 75, 77, 112-113
    Late reading, 26
    Records, 48-52
    Sample proposal to schools, 53-56
    Schedule, 14, 17-18, 26, 37, 40-43, 56
    State Laws and regulations, 29-30, 52
    Unfamiliar subjects, 43-47
    Working Parents, 12-15
The Homeschooling Almanac, 15
The Homeschooling Book of Answers, 15
Homeschooling For Excellence, 38, 60
The Homeschooling Handbook, 15
Homeschooling On A Shoestring, 55
Homeschooling Today, 15, 97

Homeschooling: Perspectives, 10
How Children Fail, 4, 55
How Children Learn, 4, 6, 55
I Learn Better By Teaching Myself, 55
In Their Own Way, 43, 55

Learning:
    And Play, 21-23, 47
    Different paces, 17-21, 45
    Different evaluations, 56
Learning All the Time, 55
A Life Worth Living: Selected Letters Of John Holt, 4
Living Is Learning Curriculum Guides, 31
The London Times, 47

Mathematics, 21-23, 70, 72
Moore Report International, 15, 98
A Mother's Letters to a Schoolmaster, 66-71

Occupational Outlook Handbook, 61

Peterson's Guide to Independent Study, 61
Practical Homeschooling, 15, 98
Private School, 29, 31, 78
Public School, 1-2, 18, 30, 44, 46

Reading, 17, 26-27, 30, 56, 74
Real Lives: Teenagers Who Don't Go To School, 16
The Relationship/Washington's Homeschoolers, 24

School at home, 8, 17, 34-35
The School In the Home, 65-66
A Sense of Self: Homeschooled Adolescent Girls, 16
Socialization, 8-11

Taking Charge Through Homeschooling, 15
Teach Your Own: A Hopeful Path for Education, 5, 55
Teaching:
    Certification, 24-25, 29
    Clubs, 9, 18, 30, 37, 42-46, 111, 116
    Differences from classroom, 2, 18, 24, 43
    Sharing with other parents, 18, 32
    Techniques, 2-3, 7-8, 19-28, 32, 34, 37-40, 43-47

The Teaching Home, 5, 15, 98
The Teenage Liberation Handbook, 10, 16
Typical Course of Study, K–12, 31

Unschooling, 3, 8, 15, 35-37, 84, 87, 92-93, 96
The Unschooling Handbook, 15

What Do I Do Monday?, 55
What Every First Grader Needs to Know, 31
Writing, 41, 51, 56
Writing Because We Love To, 16

Young Children Learning, 24